Seeing Blood and Water

Seeing Blood and Water

A Narrative-critical Study of John 19:34

SEBASTIAN A. CARNAZZO

☙PICKWICK *Publications* · Eugene, Oregon

SEEING BLOOD AND WATER
A Narrative-critical Study of John 19:34

Copyright © 2012 Sebastian A. Carnazzo. All rights reserved. Except for brief quotations in critical publications or reviews, no part of this book may be reproduced in any manner without prior written permission from the publisher. Write: Permissions, Wipf and Stock Publishers, 199 W. 8th Ave., Suite 3, Eugene, OR 97401.

Pickwick Publications
An Imprint of Wipf and Stock Publishers
199 W. 8th Ave., Suite 3
Eugene, OR 97401

www.wipfandstock.com

ISBN 13: 978-1-61097-941-2

Cataloging-in-Publication data:

Carnazzo, Sebastian A.

Seeing blood and water : a narrative-critical study of John 19:34 / Sebastian A. Carnazzo.

xii + 112 p. ; 23 cm. — Includes bibliographical references and index.

ISBN 13: 978-1-61097-941-2

1. Bible. N.T. John, XIX, 34—Criticism, Narrative. I. Title.

BS2615.2 C25 2012

Manufactured in the U.S.A.

Table of Contents

Acknowledgments · vii
Abbreviations · ix

1 Preliminary Issues · 1
Introduction
Problem and Background
Purpose and Methodology of the Present Study
Conclusion

2 John 19:34 in Its Literary and Cultural Context · 20
Introduction
Textual Tradition of 19:31–37
Translation of 19:31–37
Literary Structure of 19:31–37
Blood in the Cultural Milieu of the Fourth Gospel
Water in the Cultural Milieu of the Fourth Gospel
Conclusion

3 Blood in the Gospel Preceding John 19:34 · 31
Introduction
Born Not of Blood (1:13)
Blood of Life (6:53–56)
Eucharistic Imagery
The Son of Man
Blood
Conclusion

4 Water in the Gospel Preceding John 19:34 · 41
Introduction
Ritual Purification and John's Baptism with Water (1:26, 31, 33)

Table of Contents

        Water in Jars for Jewish Rituals of Purification (2:7–9)
        A New Birth and Purification by Water and the Spirit (3:5)
        John's Baptism, Ritual Purification, and the Water at Aenon (3:23)
        Drinking Living Water without a Bucket (4:7–15)
        Drinking Living Water and the Holy Spirit (7:37–39)
        Purification of the Disciples by a Washing with Water (13:5)
        Conclusion

5   The Interpretation of John 19:34 · 62
        Introduction
        The Piercing of Jesus' Side and the Fulfillment of Scripture (19:31–37)
        Blood in the Culture and Gospel Preceding 19:34
        Water in the Culture and Gospel Preceding 19:34
        The Meaning of Blood and Water in 19:34
        Sacramental Symbolism
        Conclusion

6   Closing Remarks · 82
        Introduction
        Summary of the Study
        Contributions to Critical Research
        Suggestions for Future Study
        Conclusion

        Bibliography · 93
        Scripture Index · 105

Acknowledgments

THE PRESENT WORK IS a modified version of my doctoral dissertation defended in 2011 at the Catholic University of America. Thus, the following persons who assisted me in that original endeavor must be acknowledged by name: First, and foremost, the director of the dissertation, John Paul Heil, S.S.D., who spent countless hours carefully reviewing and correcting each chapter, and who guided me throughout the whole writing process like the diligent captain at the helm of an unwieldy ship, steadily directing it forward to the distant shore; the reader Frank J. Matera, Ph.D., who did much to bring me to candidacy through his direction of my doctoral comprehensive exam preparation and whose reading, thoughtful criticisms of content, and careful correcting of each chapter have been invaluable; the reader Francis T. Gignac, D.Phil., who taught me the Greek language, first instructed me in the Fourth Gospel through in-class readings of the Greek text, trained me in the art and science of textual criticism, guided me throughout the whole doctoral program, and whose reading, meticulous guidance in *CBQ* style, and careful correcting of each chapter have been priceless; my former professor Francis J. Moloney, D.Phil., who, during my coursework, first introduced me to narrative-criticism and its value in the study of the Fourth Gospel; my parents William S. Carnazzo M.D., and Araceli L. Carnazzo M.D., who assisted me financially throughout my schooling, taught me the Christian Faith, and for whose constant paternal love and guidance throughout my life I am eternally indebted; my father-in-law Thomas F. Kalil, J.D., who spent numerous hours editing the whole dissertation with a careful eye to the logic of the argument, continuously worked by my side as a true παράκλητος, and who gave me fatherly advice and encouragement to the end; my friend and colleague John Pepino, Ph.D., who edited multiple chapters, encouraged constantly, and assisted me in hours of research of patristic and classical sources; the Rev. José Zepeda and Mrs. Alecia Rolling who assisted in Spanish and German translation

Acknowledgments

issues, respectively; my sister-in-law Linda Carnazzo, who patiently and carefully edited the first chapter and set me in the right direction for the rest of the study; my brother Sabatino Carnazzo, M.A., who through his brotherly love, knowledge of Scripture, and constant encouragement has been an inspiration throughout the whole writing process; and finally and most importantly my wife Leila, who edited chapters, made sacrifices in our family life, and who through her continual encouragement, love, and commitment caused me to complete the dissertation and now this present work as well.

Abbreviations

AB	*Anchor Bible*
ABD	*D. N. Freedman et al. (eds.), Anchor Bible Dictionary*
ABRL	*Anchor Bible Reference Library*
AnBib	Analecta biblica
Arch	*Archaeology*
AusBR	*Australian Biblical Review*
BARev	*Biblical Archaeology Review*
BDAG	W. Bauer, W. F. Arndt, and F. W. Gingrich (3d ed.; rev. by F. W. Danker), Greek-English Lexicon of the NT
BHS	Biblia Hebraica Stuttgartensia
BNTC	Black's NT Commentaries
BSac	*Bibliotheca Sacra*
BT	*Bible Translator*
BTB	*Biblical Theology Bulletin*
BZ	*Biblische Zeitschrift*
CahRB	Cahiers de la Revue biblique
CBET	Contributions to Biblical Exegesis and Theology
CBQ	*Catholic Biblical Quarterly*
CBQMS	CBQ, Monograph Series
CCL	*Corpus Christianorum, series latina*
ConBNT	Coniectanea biblica, New Testament
CSEL	Corpus scriptorium ecclesiasticorum Latinorum
EBib	Études bibliques

Abbreviations

EPRO	Études préliminaires aux religions orientales
GCS	Die griechischen christlichen Schriftsteller
HALOT	W. Baumgartner et al., *Hebrew and Aramaic Lexicon of the Old Testament*
HTKNT	Herders theologischer Kommentar zum Neuen Testament
HTR	*Harvard Theological Review*
Int	*Interpretation*
ITQ	*Irish Theological Quarterly*
JBL	*Journal of Biblical Literature*
JQR	*Jewish Quarterly Review*
JSJ	*Journal for the Study of Judaism in the Persian, Hellenistic, and Roman Periods*
JSNT	*Journal for the Study of the New Testament*
JSNTSup	JSNT, Supplement Series
JSOT	*Journal for the Study of the Old Testament*
JSOTSup	JSOT, Supplement Series
JTS	*Journal of Theological Studies*
MTZ	*Münchener theologische Zeitschrift*
Neot	*Neotestamentica*
NovT	*Novum Testamentum*
NovTSup	Novum Testamentum, Supplements
NTS	*New Testament Studies*
OTS	Oudtestamentische studiën
PG	Patrologia graeca [=Patrologiae cursus completus: Series graeca]. Edited by J.-P. Migne. 162 vols. Paris, 1857–1886
PL	Patrologia latina [=Patrologiae cursus completus: Series latina]. Edited by J.-P. Migne. 217 vols. Paris, 1844–1864
RB	*Revue biblique*
ResQ	*Restoration Quarterly*
SBFLA	*Studii biblici franciscani liber annuus*

Abbreviations

SBLDS	SBL Dissertation Series
SBT	Studies in Biblical Theology
SC	Sources chrétiennes
SJT	*Scottish Journal of Theology*
SNTSMS	Society for New Testament Studies Monograph Series
SR	*Studies in Religion/Sciences religieuses*
STDJ	Studies on the Texts of the Desert of Judah
TBT	*The Bible Today*
TS	*Theological Studies*
VT	*Vetus Testamentum*
WUNT	Wissenschaftliche Untersuchungen zum Neuen Testament
ZNW	*Zeitschrift für die neutestamentliche Wissenschaft*

1

Preliminary Issues

INTRODUCTION

THE GOSPEL OF JOHN presents a number of details not contained in the Synoptic Gospels. Significant among these differences is the Johannine version of the crucifixion (19:12–42). A full understanding of this climactic narrative—the depiction of Jesus' death and the details that immediately surround this event (19:31–37)—is dependent on the interpretation of the central verse that recounts the piercing of Jesus' side and the subsequent flowing of blood and water (19:34).

PROBLEM AND BACKGROUND

The various interpretations of this verse appearing in exegetical literature from the early patristic period and into the modern era comprise a massive literary body.[1] In the ante-Nicene period, writers such as Irenaeus, Hippolytus, Tertullian, Origen, and Cyprian saw in John 19:34 the fulfillment of OT imagery such as the wilderness rock that gave water (Exod 17:1–7;

---

1. The possible allusions to the text of John 19:34 in the canon of the NT are relatively sparse, being limited to 1 John 5:6–8 and Rev 1:7. Concerning 1 John 5:6–8, see Meehan, "John 19:32–35 and 1 John 5:6–8: A Study in the History of Interpretation." For a brief discussion of the scribal addition in Matt 27:49, see the summary in Metzger, *Textual Commentary on the Greek New Testament*, 59. See also the section titled "Suggestions for Future Study" in chapter 5 below.

Num 20:2–13) and the salvific red cloth hanging from Rahab's window (Josh 2:18). They also perceived NT symbolism, such as the power of the Holy Spirit, the divinity of Jesus, the reality of his human body, the birth of the Church, symbols of baptism and Eucharist, and salvation through either the water of baptism or the blood of martyrdom.[2]

After Nicea, the vast majority of interpretations of John 19:34 did nothing more than restate what had been said before, and those few cases of further development only built with relatively minor contributions upon the exegetical foundations that had already been laid.[3] In the following period, the writers of the Middle Ages inherited this post-Nicene patristic tradition and simply passed it on to the Renaissance world with no discernable development.[4]

With the beginning of the sixteenth century, a new era in biblical studies dawned, as the role of Scripture took center stage in the debates that eventually led to the splintering of Western Christianity. However, in the theological arguments of that tumultuous period, the Gospel of John played no special role.[5] Thus, the two most monumental characters of this movement, Martin Luther and John Calvin, express knowledge of the earlier exegetical tradition concerning John 19:34 and accept it with little debate.[6]

In fact, in his commentary on Gen 49:11, Luther explicitly stated his recognition of the prior tradition that the sacraments of baptism and Eucharist "flowed from the sides of Christ."[7] Luther is significant in the

---

2. Though there are among the first-century and second-century writings a number of passages that can appear to have a relationship to John 19:34, there is no indisputable evidence of literary dependency. For a thorough discussion of the ante-Nicene exegetical literature related to John 19:34, see Maguire, *Wounded Side of Christ in Early Christian Literature*, 18–167. For a listing of the known possible references to John 19:34 in the patristic era, see the collections in Westcott, *Gospel According to St. John*, 283–86 and Malatesta, "Blood and Water," 164–81, here 179–81.

3. These minor contributions are found in the writings of John Chrysostom, Ephrem the Syrian, and Augustine of Hippo. For more discussion see Maguire, *Wounded Side of Christ in Early Christian Literature*, 168–233 and Brock, "The Mysteries Hidden in the Side of Christ," 462–72.

4. For a study of this general tendency, see McNally, *The Bible in the Early Middle Ages*, 5–13.

5. Schnackenburg, *Das Johannesevangelium*, 1. 186.

6. Philip Melanchton also wrote a commentary on John (*Enarratio in Evangelium Joannis*), but he did not address John 19:34.

7. Luther, *Commentary on Genesis 49:11* (*Werke*, 44.768). Among the three times that

exegetical history, however, as he further suggested that the imagery of John 19:34, when viewed in light of 1 John 5:6–9, is better understood concerning baptism alone, which happens through water that is "stained" and thus "sanctified by the blood of Christ."[8]

John Calvin, second only to Luther in influence during the early Reformation, also accepted the earlier sacramental interpretation of John 19:34 and even the combination of its imagery with that of 1 John 5:6–8.[9] But Calvin contributed something new to the exegetical tradition on this point when he explained that John is declaring, through the description of the flow of blood and water, that the old law regulations regarding "sacrifices and washings" are fulfilled in the sacraments of "baptism and the Lord's Supper."[10] New also is Calvin's explicit denial of any miraculous aspect to the nature of the event, interpreting the blood as naturally congealed and coming forth with the serum and the water "contained in the membrane adjoining the intestines."

In the century following Luther and Calvin, Catholic exegesis, in a Counter-Reformation, continued the scholastic model of reliance on the patristic tradition, while at the same time began to address, with an apologetic tone, the writings of the reformers. A prime example of this model is Cornelius à Lapide, who in his commentary on the Gospel, after having argued against Calvin that the event described in 19:34 was indeed miraculous, simply summarized much of what had been said before him in the patristic period.[11]

Luther refers to the piercing of Christ's side in his writings (cp. ibid., 20.777; 49. 131), this is the only place where it appears in the plural ("*sacramenta fluxerunt ex lateribus Christi*"). A piercing 'through,' creating two openings, appears as early as Prudentius who speaks of it in three of his hymns, describing the blood coming from one side and the water from the other (*De Pass. Christi*; *Peristephanon*, 8; *Kathemerion*, 9). It is unclear if there is a connection between Luther's words and those of Prudentius, but it is not out of the question given the general popularity of Prudentius's writings throughout the medieval and renaissance periods, and Luther's own interest in him (*Table Talk*, 528). Cornelius à Lapide cites Prudentius explicitly in favor of the piercing through (see n. 11 below).

8. Luther, *Commentary on 1 John 5:6* (*Werke*, 20.778).

9. Calvin, *In Evangelium Ioannes*, 19:34 (*Corpus Reformatorum*, 47.422).

10. Ibid., 421.

11. While understanding the primary reference to baptism and Eucharist, Cornelius, citing Augustine, saw also a symbolism of all sacraments (see Crampon, *Cornelii à Lapide*, 16. 1151). Of notable interest as well is Cornelius' interpretation that there were two wounds (see also n. 7 above). Cornelius, who supports his argument by citing Prudentius who also speaks of a piercing through, suggests the possibility that the spear

Seeing Blood and Water

As the polemical dust of the reformational skirmish slowly settled, Christian exegetes began to look outside the bounds of their own literature for assistance in interpretation. Philological interests led to an investigation into classical and Jewish works, as in the classic studies of John Lightfoot. Concerning the text of John 19:34, it appears that Lightfoot, though he does not state it explicitly, had Calvin's commentary in mind, as he, like Cornelius, expressly rejected the interpretation that the blood and water flowed for purely "natural reasons."[12]

Contrarily, Lightfoot argues for the more traditional position of a "preternatural" event. Acknowledging the existence of the sacramental interpretation, Lightfoot preferred, as did Calvin, an OT prefigurement in both the blood and water. In support of this interpretation, Lightfoot referred to Heb 9:19 where Moses' ratification of the covenant is described as incorporating both blood and water.[13]

Lightfoot again contributed to the exegetical tradition concerning John 19:34 when he suggested a possible connection to a tradition in rabbinic literature where it is explained that Moses struck the rock in the wilderness twice (Num 20:11) because the first time blood flowed, and only the second time water.[14] Lightfoot, further supporting his interpretation with the Pauline association of Jesus and the wilderness rock (1 Cor 10:4), concluded that the purpose of the imagery expressed in John 19:34 was to enable the audience of the Gospel to "believe that this is the true blood of the new covenant, which so directly answers the type in the confirmation of the old."[15]

After Lightfoot, many scholars of the eighteenth century, with their interest in historical issues, began to question the Fourth Gospel's historical

---

entered through the right side producing a large wound from which flowed blood and protruded through the left side from which flowed water. The water flowed from the left, Cornelius argues, since this is the location of the heart, and that the fluid came from the pericardium. For further discussion of this era and a listing of others who wrote commentaries on John, see Schnackenburg, *Das Johannesevangelium*, 1.187.

12. J. Lightfoot, *Commentary on the New Testament*, 3.439–41.

13. There is no mention of water in the narrative of Exod 24:6. If the author of Hebrews is thinking of the "washings" earlier (19:10, 14), it is not clear (cp. Lev 14:6–7; Num 19:6–9, 18, 20).

14. Ibid., 440. Lightfoot refers to *Shemoth Rabba*, which is more commonly known as *Exod. Rab.* Exod 4:9. The same idea appears also in *Tg. Onq.* Num 20:11. For more discussion of this rabbinic tradition, see the section titled "Suggestions for Future Study" in chapter 5 below.

15. Ibid., 441.

value and its connection with the Apostle John.[16] By the nineteenth century the Gospel was commonly considered devoid of any historically reliable information about the life of Jesus.[17] Throughout this period, however, commentaries on the Fourth Gospel continued to be produced.

Particularly significant among the commentaries from the latter part of the nineteenth century was that of Brooke F. Westcott, who in his commentary on John interpreted the blood and water of 19:34 as symbolic of a "double cleansing and vivifying power," where the blood referred to "natural life" and the water to "spiritual life."[18] He concluded that this "life" was an allusion to baptism and Eucharist.

Shortly after Westcott, John H. Bernard argued in his commentary that John's intention was of a purely apologetic nature.[19] Thus, according to Bernard, John described "the flow of blood and water from the pierced side of Jesus as a 'natural phenomenon,' which he specifically noted because he wished to refute the Docetic doctrines prevalent when the Gospel was composed."[20] Here we see Bernard restating an idea that had been presented as early as Irenaeus; that is, the event and its details were intended to direct one to the conclusion that Jesus possessed a truly human body.[21]

A decade later, Edwyn C. Hoskyns produced his commentary on John in which he argued that the text of 19:34 was intended to be understood as a fulfillment of John 7:38–39. Repeating the interpretation of Lightfoot, Hoskyns argued (based on Heb 9:19) that since the old covenant was inaugurated with blood and water, the "new covenant by which the old is fulfilled" is declared in like manner and is made manifest in "Christian Baptism and Eucharist."[22]

Writing during the same period as Hoskyns, Rudolf K. Bultmann, in his highly influential commentary on John, briefly argued that the mention of blood and water in 19:34 was a later "ecclesiastical redaction" to the

---

16. See the summary of this period and the critique of its literature in Schnackenburg, *Das Johannesevangelium*, 1.187.

17. Ibid., 188.

18. Westcott, *Gospel According to St. John*, 279.

19. Other significant works on the Fourth Gospel began to appear during this time, and among the most notable is that of Lagrange (*Évangile selon Saint Jean*), though his commentary on John 19:34 simply restated the scholastic style summarizations of the patristic era.

20. Bernard, *Gospel According to St. John*, 2.647.

21. See n. 2 above.

22. Hoskyns, *Fourth Gospel*, 533.

original text.²³ Thus the purpose of the imagery was, as Bultmann understood it, simply that of the redactor who intended the addition as a clear reference to the sacraments of baptism and Eucharist and nothing more.

Arguing in stark contrast to Bultmann, Robert H. Lightfoot, in his commentary on the Gospel, drew parallels between the texts of John 3:3, 6:53–56, 19:34, and Gen 1:2 and maintained that the text of John 19:34 was essential to the integrity of the Gospel's narrative. He concluded, like many before, that the symbolism pointed to the sacraments of baptism and Eucharist.²⁴

By the second part of the twentieth century, bolstered by the new interest in Johannine studies, a number of significant journal articles began to appear that dealt with the text of John 19:34 specifically.²⁵ Among some of the more important of these works was the study of M. Miguens who understood the narrative elements of the text of John 19:34 as proofs, for one knowledgeable about the subtleties of rabbinic laws, that the death of Christ, having been accompanied by the flow of blood, and thus living blood, was a valid sacrifice.²⁶ Miguens saw the water as a further support for this sacrificial interpretation based on Heb 9:19.

Following shortly after Miguen's article, J. Massyngberde Ford gave a similar interpretation, though more specifically regarding the issue of the Passover sacrifice. Her study was based upon a talmudic debate that speaks of blood flowing like water from the corpse of a crucified man. Ford argued for a new reading of John 19:34, suggesting the possibility that "St. John's καί in the phrase αἷμα καὶ ὕδωρ might be epexegetical or ascensive and a translation might read: 'And there came out immediately blood even fluid (water).'"²⁷ Though the study was not of great length or depth, Ford's contribution was significant in that she raised the possibility of reading the

---

23. Bultmann, *Das Evangelium des Johannes*, 525.

24. Lightfoot, *St. John's Gospel*, 320. Other significant works during this time were those of Dodd, *Fourth Gospel*, and Barrett, *Gospel According to St. John*. Their interpretations are similar to that of Lightfoot.

25. Foremost examples of this new movement are the inestimable contributions of the general commentaries on the Gospel in this same decade of Rudolf Schnackenburg (*Das Johannesevangelium: Einleitung und Kommentar*) and Raymond E. Brown (*The Gospel According to John*).

26. Miguens, "Salió sangre y agua," 20.

27. Ford, "Mingled Blood," 337.

text of 19:34 in a new manner, which in her view would point (as other references in the larger pericope, cp. 19:36), to the Passover lamb.[28]

The following year, Georg Richter argued, as others before him, that the imagery contained in the verse was primarily intended as an anti-Docetist polemic, so that the blood and water flowing from the side of Jesus was proof that he had a "truly human body" and that he, in fact, did truly suffer.[29]

Five years after Richter, John Wilkinson examined the anatomical and physiological details of the narrative of John 19:34 and concluded that the event was "medically possible."[30] Wilkinson's work, in its cataloguing and careful analysis of a number of earlier medical theories regarding the issue, is a valuable contribution as it put to rest the debate of historical plausibility based on medical evidence.

His exegetical conclusion, however, is the same as many before him; that is, the details of the event were intended as an anti-Docetic proof that Jesus had a genuine human body. Wilkinson saw no need to speculate further about any possible symbolism or sacramental imagery, which in his opinion "receives little or no support from the fourth gospel itself."[31]

Shortly after the appearance of Wilkinson's article, Edward Malatesta published his study of John 19:34 and concluded that the blood symbolized the death of Jesus and the water symbolized the outpouring of the Holy Spirit. Malatesta then, as others before, concluded that these symbols also pertain to the sacraments of baptism and Eucharist.[32]

The next year, Matthew Vellanickal argued that the water of John 19:34 symbolized the Spirit (based on John 7:38–39) and that the flow of blood, symbolic of Jesus' true death, is the signal in the Gospel's narrative that the promised outpouring of the Spirit has now come to pass.[33] This water is then, as Vellanickal argued, a symbol also of the sacrament of baptism.

In the following decade, Ignace de la Potterie published an article describing John 19:34 as having two distinct though mutually dependent meanings, one christological and the other pneumatological. On the one

---

28. Ibid., 338.
29. Richter, "Blut und Wasser," 14.
30. Wilkinson, "Blood and Water," 149.
31. Ibid., 171.
32. Malatesta, "Blood and Water," 175. A similar argument was forwarded a decade later by Heer, "Soteriological Significance," 33–46.
33. Vellanickal, "Blood and Water," 221–22, 228.

Seeing Blood and Water

hand, the references to fulfillment in vv. 28 and 30, while pointing back to the life of Jesus, at the same time point forward to that life being given in his death and through his blood (v. 34) for the life of the Church. On the other hand, this bestowing of life is accomplished through the Spirit, which de la Potterie understood to be signified in the water of v. 34 and Jesus' handing over of the Spirit in v. 30.[34]

A decade after de la Potterie, John P. Heil published a monograph study of the Johannine passion, death, and resurrection stories from a narrative-critical perspective.[35] In Heil's interpretation, the imagery of blood and water in John 19:34 reveals the twofold meaning of Jesus' death. The blood, a common symbol of life, reveals that Jesus' death is life-giving, while the water, a common symbol of cleansing, reveals that Jesus' death is also that which cleanses of sin.

Consequently, in Heil's understanding, this image is also part of the narrative's greater theme of the Passover in which the "cleansing water of the holy Spirit that now . . . flows together with the blood from the pierced side of the crucified Jesus empowers that blood to wash or take away the sin of the world as the sacrificial blood of the true Passover Lamb of God."[36] Heil concluded that this imagery points to the sacraments of baptism and Eucharist.[37]

In summary, from the patristic to the modern era, there has been a growing mass of exegetical literature related to John 19:34. Moreover, in the last few decades, there have been a number of significant studies published in journals along with the more recent and important monograph of Heil that have continued to contribute to the understanding of this central and climatic verse in the Fourth Gospel. However, the problem remains that there has not yet been a thorough and comprehensive literary analysis of this key verse, showing how the rich and complex symbols it contains, particularly those of blood and water, can be more fully understood and appreciated by relating them to the remainder of the Gospel's narrative.

---

34. de la Potterie, "Le Symbolisme du sang et de l'eau en Jn 19,34," 211–13.

35. Heil, *Blood and Water*, 106. Other works concerning the subject have been published since Heil; however, none has been of any great depth. See, for example, Sawyer, "Water and Blood," and Carvalho, "Symbology."

36. Heil, *Blood and Water*, 106.

37. Ibid., 108.

PURPOSE AND METHODOLOGY OF THE PRESENT STUDY

This study, in light of the problem stated above, provides a comprehensive narrative-critical analysis of John 19:34, demonstrating how the symbolism of blood and water is related to the narrative describing the death of Jesus (19:31–37), the larger crucifixion pericope (19:12–42), and the rest of the Gospel.

Over the past few decades, with the increased interest in narrative criticism and appreciation for its contributions, significant progress has been made in the field of biblical studies in general, and specifically concerning the Gospel of John.[38] The methodology of this study, building upon the recent developments in this regard, employs the tools of narrative criticism in an examination of the Gospel as a communicative process.

It is an indisputable fact of history that the text of the Gospel had a real author(s) who lived nearly two millennia ago.[39] It is also an indisputable fact of history that this text has had real readers or real audiences from the date of its completion until the present. What is disputable though, is the identity of the real author and the originally intended real audience, and thus the historically intended purpose of the Gospel.

However, the text of the Gospel contains within its narrative an implied author or narrator, and an implied reader or audience.[40] The narrator, a literary construct distinct from the real author, is the voice in the narrative perceived by its audience. The implied audience, also a literary construct, is the receiver on the other end of the narrative communication. Thus, both the narrator and the implied audience are literary creations of

---

38. Though there were earlier works that laid the preliminary groundwork in Johannine literary studies, one of the most influential developments was R. Alan Culpepper's *Anatomy of the Fourth Gospel: A Study in Literary Design* (1983). This was then followed by a number of other significant works; among the more important were Jeffrey L. Staley's *The Print's First Kiss: A Rhetorical Investigation of the Implied Reader in the Fourth Gospel* (1988) and Mark W. G. Stibbe's *John as Storyteller: Narrative Criticism and the Fourth Gospel* (1992).

39. Though there may have been earlier stages, possibly oral and written, antedating the final form of the Fourth Gospel, as many have speculated in this regard, I am referring here to the final form of the Gospel, known as the Fourth Gospel. For more discussion regarding this stage and whether it is the final stage among many or the only stage that ever existed, see Brown, *Gospel According to John*, xxiv–xxxix, lxxxi.

40. I am using here the categories and definitions of narrative criticism as outlined by Powell, *Narrative Criticism*, 19–21. For a critical discussion of these categories of Powell and their potential impact for Johannine studies in particular, see de Boer, "Narrative Criticism," 35–48.

the original author of the text, and their function, as described above, can be diagrammed as follows:[41]

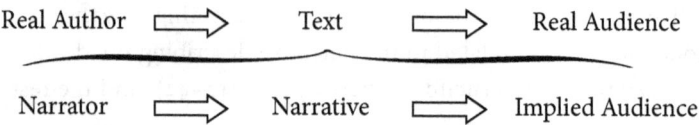

Approaching the Gospel as a communicative process emphasizes the importance of the relationship between the narrator and the implied audience. The invaluable result of this approach, as well summarized by Jack D. Kingsbury, is "to alert the interpreter both to the literary existence of the 'world of the story' and to the importance of scrutinizing it. Once one fully understands the 'world of the story,' one can then move to a reconstruction of the 'world of the evangelist.'"[42]

As such, the "world of the story" can be used as an "index" into the real world of the real author and originally intended audience, and therefore shed light on the historical context and original purpose of the Gospel.[43] This is made possible in NT narrative research since, as Francis Moloney has pointed out, "Differently from some contemporary narratives, it can generally be assumed (but never proved) that the real author *of* and the implied author *in* New Testament narratives speak with the same voice."[44] A certain kinship also applies to the receiving end of this communication, since we may also assume (but never prove), that the implied audience is reflective of the originally intended audience envisioned by the historical author, and that the historical author's vision corresponds in some degree, though the extent may be debated, to the reality of the original historical context of composition.

Suggested dates for the composition of the final form of the Gospel have ranged from as early as the middle of the first century to as late as the end of the second century.[45] Arguments for a date in the late extreme of this range have usually been based on one or more of the following points. First,

41. This diagram is based on Powell, *Narrative Criticism*, 19.
42. Kingsbury, "Reflections," 459.
43. Ibid., 459.
44. Moloney, *Gospel of John*, 16.
45. There are many hypotheses regarding possible developmental stages antedating the final form of the Fourth Gospel (see n. 39 above). The present study's methodology, however, being dependent on the narrator-audience relationship in the Gospel as we have it, is concerned only with the narrative's final form.

when compared to the Synoptic Gospels, the Gospel of John exhibits a relatively higher and more developed Christology, a fact which appears to place the composition of the Fourth Gospel at a date much later than the Synoptics. The problem with this argument is that the Pauline writings, which also exhibit a relatively higher Christology than that found in the Synoptic Gospels, are usually dated earlier than those gospels, making theological development a "precarious chronometer."[46] Furthermore, there is nothing in the theology of the Fourth Gospel, including its sacramentology, which clearly supports a compositional dating later than the first century.[47]

Another basis for a theory of late composition is the lack of the Gospel's appearance in the early second-century writings. However, there is much debate about whether this absence actually exists and, even if it does, whether or not this is the result of a late date or some other factor, such as the Gospel's early purported association with Gnosticism.[48] This suggested relationship of the Fourth Gospel with Gnosticism has itself been used as a basis for a late dating, but there is much debate about the source and date of Christian Gnosticism's origin, the veracity of its association with the Gospel, and the direction of dependency, if there be any at all.[49]

Finally, it has been argued that if the Fourth Gospel is literarily dependent on the Synoptic Gospels, and the Synoptic Gospels were composed in the latter part of the first century, as is commonly held, then the Gospel of John must have come to its final form some time later. But literary dependency between John and the Synoptics is widely disputed, and the majority of scholars now attribute similarities between John and the Synoptics to other factors.[50]

Therefore, the arguments for a late date of the final form of the Fourth Gospel, while worthy of consideration, having had much influence over the past century, are, in the final analysis, based solely on questionable theoretical chronologies of Christian theological developments, arguments from silence regarding second-century writings, and highly contested theories of the Fourth Gospel's dependency on other NT literature and Gnosticism.

---

46. Brown, *Gospel According to John*, lxxx.
47. Ibid., lxxxi.
48. For a discussion of this issue, see Pollard, *Johannine Christology*, 26–33.
49. Brown, *Gospel According to John*, lxxxii.
50. For a thorough history of the debate, see Smith, *John among the Gospels*. For the present study's position on the relationship of the Fourth Gospel to the Synoptics, see n. 80 below.

Seeing Blood and Water

A further consideration is that any hypothesis for a date of composition must take into account two boundary markers that appear to restrict the latest tenable date. First, Tatian's *Diatessaron*, composed ca. 175, treats the Fourth Gospel as being at least equal in authority to the Synoptics. As such, the Gospel was likely composed long enough before this date to acquire a level of acceptance that would justify Tatian assigning it such a status.[51]

Another significant late boundary marker is the existence of an early manuscript fragment containing John 18:31–33, 37–38. This fragment of the Gospel, known as Rylands Papyrus 457 or P52, is commonly argued to be no older than A.D. 125.[52] If this date is anywhere near accurate, and one allows for a twenty-five year margin of error, then one can reasonably conclude, assuming that P52 is a copy and not the autograph itself, that the Gospel was likely composed before A.D. 150.[53]

While external evidence limits the late extreme date, internal details also establish boundaries as to the earliest possible date. In the epilogue of the Gospel, the narrator speaks about Peter's martyrdom as if it had already taken place (21:18–19). If the interpretation of this passage is correct, and Peter died in the late 60s, then at least the epilogue must have been written after this time.[54]

Therefore, based upon the least ambiguous internal and external boundary restrictions governing the possible date of composition, it appears that the final form of the Gospel came into existence no earlier than the late 60s and no later than A.D. 150. A detail that has been thought to assist in closing this gap is the further information in the epilogue that appears to indicate that the Beloved Disciple, who is said to be the primary

---

51. Brown, *Gospel According to John*, lxxxiii.

52. Though leading papyrologists initially dated P52 to have originated sometime in the first half of the second-century (see discussion in Metzger, *Text of the New Testament*, 38–39), "the consensus has come in recent years to regard 125 as representing the later limit" (Aland and Aland, *Text of the New Testament*, 85). The present study, however, taking into account the caution warranted by some recent criticisms of the consensus (e.g. Nongbri, "The Use and Abuse of P52," 23–48) provides for the possibility of at least a twenty-five year margin of error beyond this date.

53. The fact that P52 was discovered in Egypt has been suggested by some to be evidence that drives the latest possible date of composition even earlier; however, the issue is complicated by questions concerning the Gospel's location of composition, the literary and temporal degree of relationship between the autograph and the manuscript fragment, and the manuscript's own location of composition.

54. Brown, *Gospel According to John*, lxxxv.

source behind the text, had already out lived the other eyewitnesses and, as has been interpreted by some, was either dying at the time of composition of the Gospel, or was possibly already dead (21:22–23).[55] However, this information is not as helpful as it may appear at first glance, as there is much debate about the meaning of the passage, the historical identity of the Beloved Disciple, and his degree of relationship to the composition of the Gospel.[56]

Traditionally, the Beloved Disciple has been identified as John, son of Zebedee, but this identification has not gone unchallenged. Some have suggested that the Beloved Disciple is simply a narrative symbol of the ideal disciple with no particular historical reality; but there is little evidence to support this speculation.[57] Others have proposed alternative historical figures such as Lazarus, John Mark, John the Presbyter, or some other lesser-known disciple of Jesus.[58] But all of these proposals raise more questions than they answer.[59]

Concerning the internal evidence, the Beloved Disciple is the closest disciple to Jesus in the Gospel. Elsewhere in the NT, there is evidence that John was not only one of the twelve but also one of the closer three disciples (Matt 17:1; Mark 5:37; 9:2; 14:33; Luke 8:51; 9:28; see also Gal 2:9). The Beloved Disciple is closely associated with Peter, and in the Synoptics there is an exclusive association of Peter and John (Luke 22:8). This association is even more prominent in Acts (3–4; 6:14).[60] Thus, considering the internal evidence, the identification of the Beloved Disciple with John, the son of Zebedee, seems to be the most plausible option.[61]

---

55. For example, Brown argues, based on his interpretation of the epilogue regarding the death of the Beloved Disciple (21:22–24), that the outermost limits of possible compositional dates is A.D. 75 to 110, and that there is a strong likelihood that it occurred between 90 and 100, and even possibly ca. 100 (*Gospel According to John*, lxxxv–lxxxvi).

56. For an analysis of the Beloved Disciple and a cataloging of this character's appearances and function in the Gospel narrative, see Brown, *Gospel According to John*, xcii–xciv. For an alternate interpretation of the meaning of John 21:22–23, see Bauckham, *Jesus and the Eyewitnesses*, 367.

57. Brown, *Gospel According to John*, xciv–xcv.

58. For a discussion of the plausibility of Lazarus or John Mark, see ibid., xcv–xcvii. For arguments in favor of John the Presbyter, see Hengel, *Johannine Question*; and the more forceful argument by Bauckham, "Beloved Disciple," 21–44.

59. Brown, *Gospel According to John*, xcviii.

60. For more evidence in favor of the Beloved Disciple as John, the son of Zebedee, see ibid., xcvi–xcviii.

61. Ibid., xcviii.

Seeing Blood and Water

The earliest known unambiguous external witness to the authorship of the Gospel comes from Irenaeus, who states that after the other gospels had been written, John the disciple of the Lord, "who leaned into his bosom," published his own Gospel in Ephesus and remained in Asia until the time of Trajan (*Adv. Haer.* 2.22.5; 3.1.1).[62] It appears that Irenaeus is referring here to John the apostle and son of Zebedee, whom he identifies as the one who "leaned into his bosom," thus equating him with the Beloved Disciple (John 13:23; 21:20). Though there is debate about Irenaeus's historical witness, as Raymond E. Brown concluded regarding the external evidence, "it is fair to say that the only ancient tradition about the authorship of the Fourth Gospel for which any considerable body of evidence can be adduced is that it is the work of John, the son of Zebedee."[63] Thus, as Brown also initially concluded further, "the combination of external and internal evidence associating the Fourth Gospel with John, the son of Zebedee makes this the strongest hypothesis, if one is prepared to give credence to the Gospel's claim of an eyewitness source."[64]

But even if one were to grant this identification, based on the weight of the internal and external evidence, the question remains concerning the relation of the Beloved Disciple/John the son of Zebedee to the final form of the Gospel. The Gospel's epilogue says, "This is the disciple who is bearing witness concerning these things and who wrote these things, and we know that his witness is true" (John 21:24). If the Beloved Disciple is the author of the Gospel, then who is the "we" in this passage and what if any role did the subject of the "we" have in the Gospel's final form?

Some have argued that the Beloved Disciple is the 'final' redactor of the Gospel, and this passage from the epilogue, when properly understood, poses no problem for this identification, even taking into account the plural

---

62. There are other possible allusions to the Gospel and Johannine authorship among earlier writings, especially those of Gnostic origin, but their ambiguous nature and the possibility that they are references to an earlier stage of composition significantly weaken their value in this matter. For a discussion of the issue, see Culpepper, *Son of Zebedee*, 107–38.

63. Brown, *Gospel According to John*, xcii.

64. Ibid., xcviii. Brown changed his opinion in later publications. In his introductory work on the NT Brown states, "[O]ther scholars (with whom I agree) theorize that the Beloved Disciple was a minor figure during the ministry of Jesus, too unimportant to be remembered in the more official tradition of the Synoptics" (Brown, *Introduction to the New Testament*, 369). See also the later and similar conclusions in the posthumously published Brown, *Introduction to the Gospel of John*, 189–96. However, he does not provide in either of these works any clear explanation of why he abandons his former position.

Preliminary Issues

"we."⁶⁵ Many others, however, based on a number of ancient witnesses to a tradition that someone other than John the apostle participated in rendering its final form, argue for a distinction between the Beloved Disciple/John the son of Zebedee and the subject of the "we" in this passage from the epilogue.⁶⁶ Those who argue for this distinction posit a number of possible historical identities.⁶⁷

Describing the state of the debate over this question, Jerome H. Neyrey in his recently published commentary declared: "Despite the best labors of Johannine scholarship, we are still uncertain who the author is or where and when the document was written and revised."⁶⁸ Thus, given the fact that any attempt to identify positively the subject of the "we" must be admitted to be speculative, the present study avoids making any further conclusion regarding this subject other than that the final author(s) or redactor(s), if distinct from the Beloved Disciple, was most likely a close associate of the Beloved Disciple/John the son of Zebedee and, from what can be gathered from the narrative, had a good knowledge of first-century Palestinian geography, Jewish festal cycles, OT literature, Israelite and Greco-Roman theology and politics and, most importantly for the present study, a considerable education and artistic talent in first-century literary design.⁶⁹ Beyond that, the only other detail that might be safely assumed from the narrative about its authorship is that the subject of the "we" was probably also a significant member(s) of the local ecclesial community from which the Gospel came.⁷⁰

The popular perception of this community, commonly referred to as the "Johannine community," owes its present image to two major influences

---

65. Bauckham, "Beloved Disciple," 27–31. See also his subsequent and lengthier discussion of the issue in *Jesus and the Eyewitnesses* (pp. 358–83) and particularly where he deals with the use of a plural in reference to a singular subject (pp. 369–83).

66. For a discussion of these witnesses, see Brown, *Gospel According to John*, xcix.

67. Many recent arguments have been made in favor of John the Presbyter. See the discussion in Culpepper, *Son of Zebedee*, 297–307. For arguments disassociating the Gospel from John, the son of Zebedee, and instead with John the Presbyter alone, see Bauckham, "Beloved Disciple," 21–27.

68. Neyrey, *Gospel of John*, 2.

69. For more discussion of these narrative categories in relation to the authorship of the Gospel, see Neyrey, *Gospel of John*, 2–5.

70. Concerning the location of this community, as Brown declared: "The question of the place of the Gospel's composition is not an extremely important one; but there is nothing in the internal evidence to give major support to any other theory than that which has ancient attestation; namely, that the Gospel was composed at Ephesus" (*Gospel According to John*, civ).

in recent decades.[71] The first and most formative of these influences was the publication of a number of Johannine studies, many from a sociological perspective, that perceived the Gospel as a literary window with a view of the community that produced it. Accordingly, many of the apparently historical stories about Jesus in the Fourth Gospel were actually allegorical versions of historical events in the life of the Johannine community.[72]

This manner of reading the Gospel projected an image of a community in crisis. The crisis was perceived to be the result of the community's own unorthodox version of Christianity that isolated it from the rest of the Christian world and the developing rift between Christians and Jews beginning in the second half of the first century, a rift that eventually resulted in the expulsion of Jewish Christians from the synagogues and their official excommunication following the council of Jamnia and the institution of the *Eighteen Benedictions*.[73]

This image of the Johannine community was further fostered by the concurrent discovery of the Dead Sea Scrolls, as many of the scholarly attempts to reconstruct the community behind them projected an image of a heterodox isolationist Jewish sect, an image that seemed to give historical plausibility to the developing perception of the hypothetical Johannine community.[74]

This direction of Johannine studies, focusing so intensely on the sociological reconstruction of the Johannine community and its subsequent influence on the formation of the Gospel, has not gone unchallenged. One of the most fundamental criticisms has been that the reconstruction of the hypothetical Johannine community and its description as a community

---

71. The analysis presented here is a summary of that argued by Kysar, "Whence and Whither," 65–81.

72. Though other publications contributed to this new movement, the most influential were Raymond E. Brown's commentary on the Gospel, published in 1966 and his later work, *The Community of the Beloved Disciple* in 1979; the study of J. Louis Martyn, *History and Theology in the Fourth Gospel* in 1968; and Wayne A. Meeks, "The Man from Heaven in Johannine Sectarianism," in 1972. See the similar analysis of the influence of these publications in Culpepper, *Son of Zebedee*, 309–12.

73. The *Eighteen Benedictions* is part of the synagogue service from the late first to early second century. The twelfth "benediction" has often been taken as a condemnation of Christians. For a discussion of the issue, see the reference at n. 76 below.

74. For a discussion of these developments in relation to Johannine studies and particularly the contributions of Brown in this regard, see Fitzmyer, "Qumran Literature and the Johannine Writings"; and Bauckham, *Testimony of the Beloved Disciple*, 125–36.

in crisis, is based on a complex series of interdependent speculations with little if any unambiguous scientific support.⁷⁵

Further weakening the plausibility of the hypothesis for those critical of its validity is the potential loss of one of its most centrally supporting components. A number of studies have now argued that the *Eighteen Benedictions* were instituted much later than the Gospel's composition, were not universally incorporated into synagogue services, and may have had nothing at all to do with Christians.⁷⁶

While the popular hypothesis of the Johannine Community has come under increasingly significant criticism from a barrage of recent studies, the very relevance of the concept of a gospel community for a scientific study of a particular gospel is now being questioned as well. This scrutiny has arisen in response to a number of perceived problems with the popular hypothesis that a particular gospel was written specifically for the local ecclesial community of its author.⁷⁷

Therefore, given the present state of the debate over the historical plausibility and thus relevance of the community-specific hypothesis for Gospel research in general, and the rapidly disintegrating consensus regarding the characteristics and even the existence of the hypothetical Johannine community, the present study respectfully assumes an alternate position that would appear to better harmonize with the parameters of the scientifically established historical evidence. That is, although the Fourth Gospel may have been produced within the context of a specific ecclesial community, it was intended to have relevance for a more general audience.⁷⁸

Nevertheless, given this assumption, the present study also assumes that the author of the final form of the Fourth Gospel, as with the authors of the other Gospels, had his own unique image of the immediately surrounding and distantly outlying world. It was from this unique vantage that he envisioned a profile or portrait of his potential audience. This portrait

---

75. Kysar, "Whence and Whither," 70–73. See also Hägerland, "John's Gospel."

76. See the critical analysis and discussion in Visotzky, "Methodological Considerations."

77. The most influential publication in this regard was that of Bauckham, "For Whom Were Gospels Written?" 9–48. For a criticism of Bauckham, see Sim, "Response to Bauckham," 3–27; and Mitchell, "Patristic Counter-Evidence," 36–79. For a summary of the early stages of the debate, see Klink, "State of the Question," 60–85.

78. For arguments in favor of this middle-road position between the community-specific hypothesis and Bauckham's arguments for an "indefinite" audience, see Sim, "Response to Bauckham," 24.

may be reconstructed by a careful analysis of the Gospel narrative's introduction, explanation, and treatment of the particulars of such categories as persons, places, languages, Judaism, and events provided by the narrator to the implied audience.[79] The image created is a Greek-speaking Christian who is knowledgeable about the OT, major Palestinian geographical sites, and significant events in the life of Jesus,[80] but is not so clear on the more minor though relevant details that make up the unique quality of the Fourth Gospel.[81]

The purpose of the Fourth Gospel then, based upon this information regarding its authorship and intended audience, was to supply through a genre similar to a Greco-Roman biography a story about the life of Jesus of Nazareth,[82] in order to provide clarity regarding the various topics emphasized by the Gospel. Through this clarification and the attendant exhortation, it was intended to strengthen and encourage the faith of the Christian audience who might receive it. In short, it was written so that the Christian may believe that Jesus is the Christ, the Son of God, and that believing may have life in his name (John 20:31).[83]

CONCLUSION

The present chapter has provided a general introduction to the history of interpretation of John 19:34, the problem this verse poses for Johannine research, and the purpose and methodology of the present study. Following

---

79. For a detailed analysis of the categories and the resultant portrait produced, see Culpepper, *Anatomy*, 211–27. See also Moloney, *Gospel of John*, 17.

80. The present study assumes that the author of the Fourth Gospel may have been aware of the story about Jesus as it found expression in the Synoptic tradition, but not necessarily that he had direct contact, or that he assumed his intended audience had direct contact, with one or more of what eventually became the canonical Synoptic Gospels.

81. As Moloney has described the Fourth Gospel: "It is Greek and Jewish, and its language, background, and theological point of view would resonate within a number of worldviews" (*Gospel of John*, 6).

82. Concerning the possibility of the relationship of the Gospels to this genre, see Burridge, *Gospels*. Regarding this genre and the Fourth Gospel specifically, see Bauckham, *Testimony of the Beloved Disciple*, 93–112.

83. See the similar conclusion of Culpepper, *Anatomy*, 225–26. For a discussion of the manuscript variation on this verse, the grammatical problems regarding verbal aspect, and support for the present interpretation, see Brown, *Introduction to the Gospel of John*, 152, 182.

this introduction, the study provides, in chapter 2, a discussion of the manuscript tradition of John 19:31–37, the pericope in which this verse appears, and offers an English translation along with an analysis of its literary structure. Chapter 2 also includes an investigation of the symbolic significance of the images of blood and water in the cultural milieu of the Gospel's intended audience. To further shed light on the imagery in John 19:34, the study then proceeds, in chapters 3 and 4, with an examination of the use of the words "blood" and "water" in the Gospel preceding 19:34. After this examination, the study then continues, in chapter 5, with a focused analysis of 19:34 in its immediate literary context (19:31–37). Finally, chapter 6 concludes the study with a summary of its findings and an explanation of how the study contributes to the research of Johannine literature. The chapter then closes with some suggestions for future research.

2

John 19:34 in Its Literary and Cultural Context

INTRODUCTION

THE PREVIOUS CHAPTER EXAMINED the history of interpretation of John 19:34, the significance of this verse for Johannine research, the purpose of this study, and its methodology. The present chapter provides a discussion of the manuscript tradition of John 19:31–37, the pericope in which this verse appears, and offers an English translation along with an analysis of its literary structure. The chapter also provides a discussion of the symbolic value of blood and water in the cultural milieu of the Fourth Gospel and demonstrates how this symbolic value influences the intended audience.

TEXTUAL TRADITION OF 19:31–37

The Greek text of John 19:31–37 with minor alteration is presented here as it appears in NA²⁷:[1]

31 Οἱ οὖν Ἰουδαῖοι, ἐπεὶ παρασκευὴ ἦν, ἵνα μὴ μείνῃ ἐπὶ τοῦ σταυροῦ τὰ σώματα ἐν τῷ σαββάτῳ, ἦν γὰρ μεγάλη ἡ ἡμέρα

---

1. In John 19:35, the text of NA²⁷ has πιστεύ[σ]ητε. This is a change from the πιστεύητε of NA²⁵. I have presented 19:35 here with πιστεύητε in accord with NA²⁵ for the reasons explained below. In the rest of this study, unless otherwise noted, quotations of the Greek text of the NT are taken from NA²⁷.

ἐκείνου τοῦ σαββάτου, ἠρώτησαν τὸν Πιλᾶτον ἵνα κατεαγῶσιν αὐτῶν τὰ σκέλη καὶ ἀρθῶσιν.

32 ἦλθον οὖν οἱ στρατιῶται καὶ τοῦ μὲν πρώτου κατέαξαν τὰ σκέλη καὶ τοῦ ἄλλου τοῦ συσταυρωθέντος αὐτῷ·

33 ἐπὶ δὲ τὸν Ἰησοῦν ἐλθόντες, ὡς εἶδον ἤδη αὐτὸν τεθνηκότα, οὐ κατέαξαν αὐτοῦ τὰ σκέλη,

34 ἀλλ᾽ εἷς τῶν στρατιωτῶν λόγχῃ αὐτοῦ τὴν πλευρὰν ἔνυξεν, καὶ ἐξῆλθεν εὐθὺς αἷμα καὶ ὕδωρ.

35 καὶ ὁ ἑωρακὼς μεμαρτύρηκεν, καὶ ἀληθινὴ αὐτοῦ ἐστιν ἡ μαρτυρία, καὶ ἐκεῖνος οἶδεν ὅτι ἀληθῆ λέγει, ἵνα καὶ ὑμεῖς πιστεύητε.

36 ἐγένετο γὰρ ταῦτα ἵνα ἡ γραφὴ πληρωθῇ· ὀστοῦν οὐ συντριβήσεται αὐτοῦ.

37 καὶ πάλιν ἑτέρα γραφὴ λέγει· ὄψονται εἰς ὃν ἐξεκέντησαν.

The text of John 19:31–37 is remarkably stable in the extant manuscript tradition and manifests only two noteworthy variants. First, the entirety of 19:35 is absent from the fifth-century Latin codex Palatinus and the sixth-century Latin codex Fuldensis.[2]

Since the Greek manuscript tradition, the other Latin witnesses, and the rest of the versions overwhelmingly attest to this verse, and given the verse's characteristically Johannine style, it can safely be assumed, against Palatinus and Fuldensis, that 19:35 is authentic.[3]

The second noteworthy variant concerns the last word of 19:35. It is the present subjunctive πιστεύητε in Vaticanus, the first hand of Sinaiticus, Athous Lavrensis, and Origen. The second corrector of Sinaiticus, as well as Alexandrinus and most other external witnesses, however, have the aorist subjunctive πιστεύσητε.

If the aorist subjunctive πιστεύσητε is original and the author intended it to carry an ingressive sense, it would seem that the verse is addressed to a non-Christian audience that might come to believe upon hearing the Gospel. If the present subjunctive πιστεύητε is original, assuming the author intended the present to convey continuous aspect, it could be

---

2. NA[27].

3. Bernard, *Gospel According to St. John*, 2. 649. See also Brown, *Gospel According to John*, 2. 936.

understood that the verse is addressed to a Christian audience that they may persevere in belief.

As described in detail in the previous chapter, the present study assumes that the Gospel was composed for a Christian audience with the intention of strengthening faith. As also discussed previously, this assumption is based upon a number of internal indications. While this does not conclusively rule out the possibility that πιστεύσητε is original, as it is possible that the author used the aorist subjunctive but did not intend an ingressive sense, it gives further support, along with the stronger external attestation, that the present subjunctive πιστεύητε is more likely original.[4]

TRANSLATION OF 19:31–37

The following translation attempts to convey the exegetically essential elements of the Greek text within the boundaries of modern idiomatic English style.

31 Since it was the Preparation Day, that the bodies might not remain on the cross during the Sabbath, for that Sabbath was an especially solemn day, the Jews asked Pilate that the legs of those who had been crucified be broken and their bodies be taken away.

32 So the soldiers came and broke the legs of one and then of the other who had been crucified with him.

33 But when they came to Jesus and saw that he was already dead, they did not break his legs.

34 Instead, one of the soldiers stabbed his side with a spear, and immediately there came out blood and water.

35 The one who saw this has testified that also you may believe. His testimony is true, and he knows that he tells the truth.

36 This happened that the Scripture passage might be fulfilled, "None of its bones shall be crushed."

37 Also another Scripture passage says, "They shall look at him whom they have pierced."

---

4. For a similar analysis of the issue, see Brown, *Introduction to the Gospel of John*, 152, 182–83.

John 19:34 in Its Literary and Cultural Context

There is an intentional differentiation in the English word choice to preserve the distinction that exists in the Greek text between the request of the Jews in 19:31, the action of the soldiers in 19:32, and the fulfillment of the Scripture passage in 19:36. In 19:31 and 19:32, the request that the legs be broken, and the action of the soldiers are both described with the aorist of the Greek verb κατάγνυμι. In 19:36 the verb from the fulfilled Scripture passage is the future passive of συντρίβω. Though these two verbs overlap in their range of meaning, the distinction exists in the text. The translation preserves this distinction for consistency.[5]

Similarly, the action of the soldier in 19:34 is described with the aorist of the Greek verb νύσσω, whereas the Greek verb in the fulfilled Scripture passage in 19:37 is the aorist of ἐκκεντέω. Again, while these verbs may overlap in their range of meaning, the distinction exists in the text. Thus, here as well, the translation preserves the distinction for consistency.[6]

LITERARY STRUCTURE OF 19:31–37

The body of the Gospel, framed by a prologue (1:1–18) and an epilogue (21:1–25), may be divided schematically into two major sections commonly called the Book of Signs (1:19–12:50) and the Book of Glory (13:1—20:31).[7] The latter section is composed of three parts: the Final Discourse (13:1—17:26), the Passion (18:1—19:42), and the Resurrection (20:1–29). The second of these three parts, the Passion, may be divided further into what has been titled "Jesus, the Jews, and Peter" (John 18:1-27), "Jesus, the Jews, and Pilate" (John 18:28—19:11), and "The Revelatory Death and Burial of Jesus" (19:12-42).[8]

The final section (19:12-42) comprises six scenes which can be described thematically as the Judgment (19:12-22), the Crucifixion (19:23-24), the Words at the Cross (19:25-27), the Death (19:28-30), the Piercing of Jesus (19:31-37), and the Burial (19:38-42).[9]

---

5. See also Heil, *Blood and Water*, 104.

6. See also Brown, *Gospel According to John*, 2.931.

7. Brown, *Gospel According to John*, 1.cxxxviii-cxxxix. For a reassessment of the literary boundaries of the Book of Signs and an argument for a total of seven signs culminating in the cross, see Girard, "Composition structurelle," 315-24. For a discussion of the general problem of literary structure in the Fourth Gospel and a survey of the various solutions proposed, see Mlakuzhyil, *Christocentric Literary Structure*, 5-86.

8. Heil, *Blood and Water*, 16, 45, 77.

9. See similarly ibid., 9.

The second-to-last scene, the pericope that contains 19:34, may be divided into three parts:

A The Breaking of the Legs of Those Crucified with Jesus (19:31–33)
  B The Piercing of Jesus and the Coming Forth of Blood and Water (19:34)
    C The Testimony of the Narrator (19:35)
A' The Fulfillment of a Scripture passage (19:36)
  B' The Fulfillment of another Scripture passage (19:37)

The two events, that of 19:31–33 and that of 19:34, are shown in 19:35–37 to fulfill two passages from the OT with the intention of strengthening the faith of the Gospel audience.

In order to understand how the author may have expected the imagery of blood and water in 19:34 to have this effect on the intended audience requires an examination of the use of the images of blood and water in the cultural milieu and preceding narrative of the Gospel.

BLOOD IN THE CULTURAL MILIEU OF THE FOURTH GOSPEL

Ancient Israel perceived blood as the seat of life (Gen 9:4; Lev 17:11, 14; Deut 12:23). Since God was understood as the source of all life, particular rules governed and guarded the treatment of blood in common day-to-day activities and in the rituals of the cult of Israel.[10]

Since an animal's God-given life was in its blood, the consumption of blood or even the eating of animal flesh that had not been properly drained was prohibited (Gen 9:4; Deut 12:16, 23; 15:23; 1 Sam 14:32–35). Likewise, since humanity was made in the image of God, murder, which caused the spilling of innocent blood, was considered a particularly heinous crime (Gen 9:5–6). Thus in the case of murder, God demanded an accounting (Gen 9:5), as the blood cried out for vengeance (Gen 4:10–11; 2 Sam 21:1; Ezek 24:7–8; 35:6). This accounting for the spilling of innocent blood, or life, is described as God's special prerogative and responsibility, especially when it was the innocent blood of God's servants (Ps 79:10; 2 Macc 8:3).

---

10. Here and below, unless otherwise noted, I am summarizing the brief presentation of the topic in Spicq and Grelot, "Sang." For a thorough treatment of the subject, see Gilders, *Blood Ritual in the Hebrew Bible*.

John 19:34 in Its Literary and Cultural Context

The close relationship between blood and life gave rise to a number of cultic uses. In the Exodus the blood of a lamb or goat was smeared on the doorpost and lintel (Exod 12:7-13, 22-27). This action was probably understood to purify the doorway ritually, creating a demarcation between the outside and the inside of the house. The inside, as a result, would become a zone of purity and asylum of life, which preserved the firstborn alive for Israel.[11] In the establishment of a covenant the blood of a sacrificed animal was put on both parties, symbolizing their kinship bond of covenantal consanguinity and life.[12] This can be seen, for example, in the Sinai narrative where blood was put on the people and altar, a ritual that was also likely associated with purification (Exod 24:3-8; Zech 9:11).[13]

In the sacrificial system, the blood of an animal was used in purification for sin. Through the blood of the animal, the repentant Israelite was purified ritually and restored to life metaphorically by reestablishment of the right covenantal relationship with God. This purificatory usage appears most prominently in the ritual for the Day of Purification (Lev 16:15-21) and the basic concept that underlies the ritual is summarized as follows: "For the life of the flesh is in its blood, and I have given it to you for purification for your lives upon the altar, for it is the blood, by its life, that purifies" (17:11).[14] The association of blood with purification for sin is vividly evident in the technical term for the sacrifice for sin, which, though often

---

11. Propp, *Exodus*, 1.437. Propp sees further indication of the purgative function of the blood in the use of the hyssop, which was understood to have a naturally purifying character and appears in other clearly ritually purgative narratives (Lev 14:4, 6, 49, 51, 52; Num 19:6, 18; see also Ps 51:7). That this was the basic function of the rite may also be indicated in the similar rite in Ezekiel's temple (Ezek 45:18-20), where the purgative imagery is explicit (ibid.). For more discussion of the blood rituals in Ezekiel's temple, see Gilders, *Blood Ritual in the Hebrew Bible*, 142-57.

12. Gaster, *Myth, Legend, and Custom*, 151.

13. Propp, *Exodus*, 2.309.

14. Here and below I have used the word "purification" or "purify" in place of the more common "atonement" or "atone" (KJV, RSV, NAB, NRSV) as the former better describes the biblical concept (Milgrom, *Leviticus*, 1.255-58, 1009) and the latter has been part of a popular confusion about the meaning of sacrifice in the OT and NT alike. As Joseph A. Fitzmyer has stated, "It was not that blood shed in sacrifice pleased Yahweh; nor that the shedding of blood and ensuing death were a recompense or price to be paid. Rather, the blood was shed either to purify and cleanse objects ritually dedicated to Yahweh's service (Lev 16:15-19) or to consecrate objects or persons to that service..." (*Paul and His Theology*, 65). For the problem of the word "atonement" specifically, see ibid., 63.

Seeing Blood and Water

dynamically rendered "sin offering" in modern translations (*RSV*, *NAB*, *NRSV*), is formally translated "blood of sin" (דַּם חַטָּאת).[15]

Much of the above symbolism was adopted into the language of the Christian kerygma. The basic association between blood and life, or loss of blood and loss of life is common in the NT (Matt 23:30, 35; 27:4, 6, 8, 24, 25; Luke 11:50, 51; 13:1; Acts 1:19; 5:28; 18:6; 20:26; 22:20; Rom 3:15; Rev 6:10; 16:3, 6; 17:6; 18:24; 19:2).

Furthermore, through metaphor, echoes of Israel's sacrificial cult can be heard in a number of passages in the NT where Jesus is described as a Passover lamb (1 Cor 5:7; 1 Pet 1:19) or sacrificial animal whose death and blood, through purification for sin, gave life to the world (Rom 3:24–25; 1 Cor 10:16–18; Eph 1:7). In other places, Jesus is metaphorically described as having taken the place of the sacrificial animals on the Day of Purification, carrying his own blood into the heavenly sanctuary for the purification of sin (Heb 9:11–14, 23–28; 10:19; 12:24; 13:12; 1 Pet 1:2).[16] As it is stated in Hebrews, "Indeed, under the law almost everything is purified by blood, and apart from the shedding of blood there is no forgiveness" (9:22). A summary of this concept in the Johannine literature appears in 1 John, "The blood of Jesus purifies us of all sin" (1:7b; see also Rev 1:5; 7:14; 12:11).

Finally, and possibly most significant, is the use of the image of Jesus' death, or blood, as a sign of the New Covenant, imagery obviously intended to recall the covenantal narrative at Sinai (Matt 26:28; Mark 14:24; Luke 22:20; 1 Cor 11:25).

In summary, in the cultural surroundings of the author and intended audience of the Fourth Gospel, blood was associated first and foremost with life. In the OT, a body of literature familiar to the audience of the Gospel, this association of blood and life gave rise to a number of cultic rituals in which blood was used in purification for sin. In the NT this association of blood with life and purification for sin was adopted to speak about the life-giving death of Jesus and its metaphorically purgative character. The author would expect much of this cultural background to influence the audience when they heard about the blood in John 19:34.

---

15. See especially Exod 30:10; Lev 4:25, 34; 5:9; Ezek 45:19. All quotations of the Hebrew Bible in this study, unless otherwise noted, are taken from BHS. For more discussion about the purpose of the sin offering, see Gilders, *Blood Ritual in the Hebrew Bible*, 109–41.

16. For more discussion, see Fitzmyer, *Paul*, 62–66.

John 19:34 in Its Literary and Cultural Context

WATER IN THE CULTURAL MILIEU OF THE FOURTH GOSPEL

In the Scriptures of Israel, water is portrayed primarily as a natural cleansing mechanism and the essential life-sustaining quencher of thirst without which the land becomes arid and its plant and animal life perishes.[17] Whatever its source, whether from above or below, water was understood to be under the direct power of the God of Israel (Job 28:26; Prov 3:19-20) who causes the occasional floods (Job 12:15), determines the flow of springs and rivers (Isa 44:27; Ezek 31:15), and gives the rain in due season (Lev 26:4; Deut 11:14; 28:12; Job 5:10; Ps 104:10-16; Isa 30:23-25; Jer 5:24). Since the God of Israel is its creator and controller, water is also described as an instrument by which he bestows his blessings (Gen 27:28; Lev 26:3-10; Deut 28:12; Ps 133:3).

The cleansing quality of water (Gen 18:4; 19:2; 24:32) was the basis for its use in various sorts of ritual purifications, such as in preparation for ceremonial functions (Exod 29:4; 40:12; Lev 16:4), after having touched a dead body (Lev 11:40), after being cured of leprosy (Lev 14:8-9), and after contracting any sexual impurity (Leviticus 15). This ritual use of water's purgative character is well signified in the technical term "water of uncleanness" (מֵי נִדָּה), which was made by the mixing of, among other things, the ashes of a red heifer, hyssop, and living water (or "running water").[18]

Finally, and in many ways the coalescence of all of the symbolism noted above, the image of water appears in the eschatological picture of Israel's postexilic restoration. Then God will give the blessing of rain (Ezek 34:26) and, through this life-giving drink, cause seeds to sprout, plants to bud, and fields to be filled with their greenery (Isa 30:23-25). Deserts will become

---

17. Here and below, unless otherwise noted, I am summarizing the presentation of the topic in Boismard, "Eau." It is also noteworthy that the Greco-Roman world in the first century, though a massive cultural complex of various historical and geographical origins, shared the same natural environment with ancient Israel and thus contained within its world many of the same uses of water for sustenance of life and daily cleansing. The complexity of the engineering, function, and beauty of the Greco-Roman bathhouse is a well-known symbol of this ancient culture, see Ginouvès, *Balaneutiké*, DeLaine, "Roman Baths," 14-17, and most recently Fagan, "Bathing for Health." For the acceptance of this Greco-Roman cultural element in Israel, see the study by Eliav, "Roman Bath." For a discussion of the use of ritual cleansing in Greco-Roman religious ceremonies, see Cumont, *After Life*, 118. For associations of water with various divine personalities of the Greco-Roman pantheon, see Ferguson, *Greek and Roman Religions*, 8, 92, 96, 106.

18. Num 19:17. See also Num 19:9, 13, 20, 21; 31:23. For more discussion of the significance of ritual uncleanness in the cult of Israel, see Levine, *Numbers*, 1.457-79.

orchards (Isa 41:17–20), the wilderness a watered plain (Isa 35:6–7), and every thirst will be quenched by bubbling springs (Isa 49:10; Jer 31:9).

The climax of this eschatological image, that of the restoration of Jerusalem, is portrayed in a similar manner with a river of living water flowing forth from the city (Zech 14:8; see also Ezek 47:1–12; Joel 3:18) providing purification for all its inhabitants (Zech 13:1). In this latter image, water is a metaphor for one of the ultimate events of the messianic age—the pouring out of the Spirit for the purification and life of God's people (see also Isa 44:3–5; Ezek 36:24–27; Joel 2:28).[19]

All of the above symbolic uses of water were also common in the nascent Christian kerygma and are especially evident in the early explanations of baptism. First, throughout the gospel tradition the baptism by John appears as an integral part of the beginning of Jesus' public ministry and is described as the moment of the descent of God's Spirit upon him (Matt 3:13–17; Mark 1:9–11; Luke 3:21–22; John 1:19–34; see also Acts 10:37–38). Second, and obviously related to the Baptist's movement (John 3:22–4:3), was Christian baptism, which was understood to cause purification (1 Cor 6:11; Eph 5:26; Titus 3:5; Heb 10:22; 1 Pet 3:21) and unification of all by the Spirit of God (1 Cor 12:12–13; Titus 3:5). The action of submersion into the water and rising from it was compared to a death, burial, and rebirth, resulting in a new creation and life (Romans 6), like the new life of the nation of Israel as they crossed the Reed Sea (1 Cor 10:1–4).

In summary, the intended audience of the Fourth Gospel, well versed in the Scriptures of Israel and living in the multicultural complex of the Greco-Roman world, understood the image of water first and foremost as a daily sustenance of life and mechanism for common cleansing. The audience was aware also of the symbolic value of water in the religious context of Israel's cult where water was used for purification of ritual uncleanness. Most significantly, the audience was aware of the image of the eschatological expectations of Israel as well, where the cleansing and life-sustaining character of water was used as a metaphor for the purificatory and life-giving powers of God's Spirit. Finally, the audience's understanding of the cultic use of water for purification from uncleanness and the eschatological relationship to God's Spirit would be influenced to some degree by the

---

19. For a discussion of how the same symbolism is maintained in the intertestamental literature and the DSS, see "Water" in *Dictionary of Judaism*, 667. For a general study of the function of symbolism in the theology of Judaism, see Neusner, *Symbol and Theology*.

image of Christian baptism which is explained in the kerygma as the fulfillment of much of this imagery.[20]

CONCLUSION

The previous chapter examined the history of interpretation of John 19:34, the significance of the verse for Johannine research, the purpose of the present study, and the methodology it employs. The present chapter discussed the manuscript tradition of the text of John 19:31–37, the pericope in which this verse appears and offered an English translation of the pericope and an analysis of its literary structure. It also provided a summary of the background against which the blood and water mentioned in 19:34 was understood by the author given the cultural milieu of the Fourth Gospel's intended audience.

Blood was associated with life and purification from sin in both the OT and the early Christian kerygma. In the latter, however, there existed a particular emphasis on the blood and the life-giving death of Jesus and the metaphorical relationship to the cult of Israel. Water was associated with daily sustenance of life and cleansing in both the OT and early Christian kerygma. But of even more importance was the use for purification from ritual uncleanness, and especially in the eschatological images of God's Spirit which gave both spiritual purification and life.

Thus, at the most basic level, both blood and water have a parallel two-part symbolic value in the cultural milieu of the Fourth Gospel. Blood is associated with life and purification from sin. Water is associated with life and purification from uncleanness.

Blood	• Life
	• Purification from sin
Water	• Life
	• Purification from uncleanness

As might be expected, the symbolism of blood and water from the cultural milieu has a relationship to the use of these same terms in the Gospel. In order to demonstrate this point and to elucidate further the author's purpose in the use of these terms in 19:34, it is necessary to examine the

---

20. On the association of the Holy Spirit with purification, see Keener, *Divine Purity*.

occurrences of blood and water in the Gospel preceding 19:34. Chapter 3 examines the occurrences of blood. Chapter 4 examines the occurrences of water. Both chapters demonstrate the degree to which the symbolism from the cultural milieu influenced the Gospel.

3

Blood in the Gospel Preceding John 19:34

INTRODUCTION

THE PREVIOUS CHAPTER PROVIDED a discussion of the manuscript tradition of John 19:31–37, an English translation and diagram of its literary structure, and an analysis of the possible cultural assumptions of the intended audience regarding the imagery of blood and water in John 19:34. In so doing, chapter 2 demonstrated that blood was associated with life and purification from sin. The present chapter examines the occurrences of the word "blood" (αἷμα) in the Gospel that precede 19:34 and evaluates how the symbolic value from the cultural milieu is employed.

BORN NOT OF BLOOD (1:13)

In the Prologue of the Gospel the audience was told about the original state of the Word (λόγος), its association with God, and its involvement in creation (John 1:1–3). The audience was also told about the relationship of the Word with light and life, its conflict with darkness, and the purpose of John the Baptist (1:4–8). Then the narrator informed the audience about a problem. The world did not recognize the Word even though the world was made through it (1:9–10). When the Word came to its own homeland, even its own people did not receive it (1:11). Yet, as the narrator explains, some did receive the Word and became children of God, and it is in this explanation that the image of blood first occurs in the Gospel:

1:12–13 ὅσοι δὲ ἔλαβον αὐτόν, ἔδωκεν αὐτοῖς ἐξουσίαν τέκνα θεοῦ γενέσθαι, τοῖς πιστεύουσιν εἰς τὸ ὄνομα αὐτοῦ, 13 οἳ οὐκ ἐξ αἱμάτων οὐδὲ ἐκ θελήματος σαρκὸς οὐδὲ ἐκ θελήματος ἀνδρὸς ἀλλ' ἐκ θεοῦ ἐγεννήθησαν.

But to all who received him, who believe in his name, he gave power to become children of God, who were born, not of blood or of the will of the flesh or of the will of man, but of God.

The phrase "of blood" above is a translation of the plural prepositional phrase ἐξ αἱμάτων, which is more formally rendered "of bloods." The plural Greek form in the present context is probably a Semitism.[1] The word "blood" typically occurs in the plural in the Hebrew OT to describe either the blood flow associated with a violent death (Gen 4:10; Exod 22:1; etc..) or the blood flow associated with childbirth (Lev 12:4, 5, 7; Ezek 16:6, 9; or menstruation Lev 20:18).[2] The latter is the more likely reason for the plural given the present context of the Gospel. Because of this association of blood and birth (and even the blood of menstruation), conception was thought to be the result of the compaction of the mother's life-giving blood around the father's seed (Wis 7:2).

With such cultural associations of blood, life, conception, and birth, and the present literary context concerning birth, it is reasonable to assume that the author intended the image of a birth "from blood" (1:13) to refer to a natural birth. Since the term is mentioned, however, only by way of contrast to a birth from God (1:13b), there does not appear to be any development of the symbolic significance of blood beyond its basic cultural association with life.

BLOOD OF LIFE (6:53–56)

The next occurrence of blood in the Gospel is in the discourse on the bread of life (6:25–59). The story is set in the synagogue of Capernaum (6:24, 59) during the time of the Passover (6:4). Earlier in the story, on the previous

---

1. For a discussion concerning Semitic interference in John, see Brown, *Introduction to the Gospel of John*, 278–81.
2. *HALOT* s.v.

day, Jesus had multiplied fish and barley loaves to feed a crowd on the other side of the sea of Tiberias. The next day the crowd found Jesus in Capernaum and a debate ensued over the meaning of Ps 78:24 (John 6:31, 49, 58).[3] The psalm describes how God provided for Israel's needs throughout its history, such as giving them manna in the wilderness despite their lack of belief (Ps 78:22).

Applying the past problem described in the psalm to the present situation, Jesus states, "I am the bread of life, the one who comes to me will never hunger, and the one who believes in me will never thirst (John 6:35). The language plays off the idea of the life-sustaining nature of both the manna and the Torah by employing a saying about the Torah from the Wisdom literature of Israel (Sir 24:21).[4] An association of the manna and the Torah appears elsewhere (Deut 8:3)[5] and, Psalm 78 begins by explaining how God gave Israel the Torah, yet they failed to believe (78:5–8). The language of John 6:35, exhibiting a main theme of the Gospel, identifies Jesus as the Word of God in the flesh which, like the Torah of old, must be received and believed (1:12, 14).[6]

The narrator explains how these words of Jesus caused the crowd to murmur among themselves about Jesus' identity and human origins (6:41, 43). The image, which appears again later (6:61; 7:32), is probably intended to recall the murmurings of Israel against Moses (Exod 16:2; see also 15:24; 16:7–8; 17:3; Num 11:1; 14:2, 27, 29, 36; 16:11, 41; 17:5; 21:5; Deut 1:27; Ps 106:25).[7]

Jesus continued the discourse by referring once more to Ps 78:24, but this time adding something more: "Your ancestors ate manna in the wilderness and died" (John 6:49). From this point the discourse changes in tone. The mention of death signals the beginning of this change as Jesus informs the crowd that he will give his flesh for the life of the world (John 6:51).

---

3. For more discussion, see Freed, *Old Testament Quotations in the Gospel of John*, 11–16; and Menken, *Old Testament Quotations in the Fourth Gospel*, 47–65.

4. For a study of this verse and its relationship to the Wisdom tradition, see Maritz, "Imagery," 333–52.

5. See in particular Philo on LXX Exod 16:15–16 (*Leg.* 3:169–76). For a brief discussion of Philo's exegesis on this point, see Freed, *Old Testament Quotations in the Gospel of John*, 12–13. For an extensive analysis, see Borgen, *Bread from Heaven*.

6. For Jesus as the "perfection" of the Torah in the Fourth Gospel, see Moloney, *Gospel of John*, 40.

7. Bernard, *Gospel According to St. John*, 1.202.

Seeing Blood and Water

This caused the Jews to argue among themselves (6:52). The word "blood" occurs four times in Jesus' reply.[8]

> 6:53 εἶπεν οὖν αὐτοῖς ὁ Ἰησοῦς· ἀμὴν ἀμὴν λέγω ὑμῖν, ἐὰν μὴ φάγητε τὴν σάρκα τοῦ υἱοῦ τοῦ ἀνθρώπου καὶ πίητε αὐτοῦ τὸ αἷμα, οὐκ ἔχετε ζωὴν ἐν ἑαυτοῖς.
>
> So Jesus said to them, "Amen, amen, I say to you, unless you eat the flesh of the Son of Man and drink his blood, you do not have life in you.
>
> 6:54 ὁ τρώγων μου τὴν σάρκα καὶ πίνων μου τὸ αἷμα ἔχει ζωὴν αἰώνιον, κἀγὼ ἀναστήσω αὐτὸν τῇ ἐσχάτῃ ἡμέρᾳ.
>
> The one who eats my flesh and drinks my blood has eternal life, and I will raise him up on the last day.
>
> 6:55 ἡ γὰρ σάρξ μου ἀληθής ἐστιν βρῶσις, καὶ τὸ αἷμά μου ἀληθής ἐστιν πόσις.
>
> For my flesh is true food and my blood is true drink.
>
> 6:56 ὁ τρώγων μου τὴν σάρκα καὶ πίνων μου τὸ αἷμα ἐν ἐμοὶ μένει κἀγὼ ἐν αὐτῷ.
>
> The one who eats my flesh and drinks my blood abides in me and I in him.

As has already been demonstrated, blood was associated with life in the cultural milieu of the Gospel. Therefore, the basic association of blood and life in this passage would not surprise the intended audience. Yet, there are at least three indications that this passage is not only about life, but also death—specifically the death of Jesus.[9]

---

8. The word appears only three times in the sixth-century codex Bezae, as the clause 6:55b is omitted in that codex. However, given its early and diversified attestation, it can safely be assumed that the clause is original. Its absence in Bezae is probably due to homoioteleuton with 6:55a (Barrett, *Gospel According to St. John*, 299). John 6:55a occurs in Bezae as the last line on the page as well as the end of the lection (indicated by the appearance of τέλος). It appears that the scribe ran out of room since the column ends with βρω. The end of the word -σις is written in smaller letters below it. The scribe's rhythm of copying stopped at least to turn the page, if not to take a break. Such a pause would increase the chance of an error like homoioteleuton.

9. For a discussion of the role of the passion in the Gospel, see Collins, "John's Gospel," 181–86.

Eucharistic Imagery

The mention of flesh (6:51, 52, 53, 54, 55, 56) should recall for the audience the language of the prologue, "The word became flesh and dwelt among us" (1:14a). Shortly after the prologue, Jesus was described as the "lamb of God" (1:29). The most likely referent is the Passover lamb (see also 1 Cor 5:7; 1 Pet 1:19).[10] Taking this previous imagery into account along with the Passover setting of the present discourse, it seems likely that an allusion to the Passover lamb is intended here in the mention of the consumption of Jesus' flesh and blood. In the Exodus Passover (Exodus 12), those who killed a lamb, consumed the flesh, and put its blood on their doorposts preserved the life of their firstborn sons. If Jesus is being described here as an eschatological Passover lamb, then his imminent death is surely in view. That Jesus' death will occur on the Preparation Day for the Passover in this Gospel and is associated with a number of parallels to a Passover lamb in that narrative further supports this conclusion.

But Jesus is not a lamb, and the literal consumption of human flesh would have been repulsive to the audience of the Gospel.[11] Furthermore, in the Exodus Passover, the blood of the lamb was not consumed, but smeared on the doorposts (Exod 12:22) and the very act of consuming blood was prohibited (Gen 9:4; Deut 12:16, 23; 15:23; 1 Sam 14:32–35). It appears, therefore, that the author is assuming something significantly distinct about the audience if it is expected to perceive a Passover allusion, and the assumption is based on the reality that the intended audience *of* this story is nothing like the audience *in* the story.

The audience in the story is described as a crowd of Jews who had been fed by Jesus the previous day and are now in debate with him about his present words. The audience of the Gospel, however, is of an entirely

---

10. Brown, *Gospel According to John*, 1. 291. The interpretation of the words "lamb of God" (John 1:29, 36) has been the subject of much debate. Some have suggested a reference to the suffering servant in Isaiah (53:7, 10–12), others to the story of the binding of Isaac (Genesis 22), and still others to the sacrificial lamb of the *Tamid* offering (Exod 29:38–42). A plausible solution is that all of this imagery melded together in the later Christian kerygma and by the time of the composition of the Gospel. For a detailed listing and analysis of all the proposed referents and for an argument favoring a combination of Passover and suffering servant imagery, see Nielsen, "Lamb of God," 217–56.

11. Note, however, the interesting, though highly speculative suggestion of J. Albert Harrill, who argues based upon the expulsion theory that the language may be an appropriation of the charge of cannibalism for sectarian self-definition, in "Cannibalistic Language," 133–58.

different nature. As already discussed in chapter 1 of this study, the typical person in the intended audience of this Gospel would have been a fully initiated Greek-speaking Christian living in the last decade or two of the first century. Therefore, beyond a simple comparison of Jesus to the Passover lamb of Exodus 12, the author is most likely taking into consideration the Passover celebrated by the Christian audience that was indeed associated with the Passover death of Jesus.[12]

Though the institution of the Christian Passover appears in the synoptic tradition and the Pauline corpus (Matt 26:28; Mark 14:24; Luke 22:20; 1 Cor 10:16; 11:25–27) it is not recorded in John. However, as Francis J. Moloney has commented on this point: "If pre-Johannine Christianity shows that *at least* Eucharist and Baptism were central in early Christian worship, then it seems logical that the author of the Fourth Gospel would show that these Sacraments had their basis in the words and works of Jesus."[13]

The relationship of the Fourth Gospel to early Christian sacramentology has been the subject of much debate over the last century. At one extreme are those such as Rudolf Bultmann, who argued that the Gospel is antisacramental and that if there is any reference to early Christian sacramental praxis it is to be found only in ecclesiastical additions in 3:5 (baptism); 6:51–58 (Eucharist); and 19:34 (baptism and Eucharist).[14] At the other extreme are those, such as Oscar Cullmann, who argued that the Gospel is saturated with sacramental symbolism.[15] Thus, regardless of

---

12. The verb describing the one who eats changes after 6:53 from φαγ- to τρωγ- (6:54, 56, 57, 58). Many commentators have suggested, based upon the use of τρωγ- elsewhere, that the change is due to the author either intensifying the image of eating or making the physical image of chewing more explicit. Those who argue thus usually see some sort of eucharistic issue at play. Some, however, due to the switch of tenses in the verb from aorist (6:53) to present (6:54, 56, 57, 58) argue that the root change is due to the author's preference for τρωγ- over εσθ- in the present tense. Both positions attempt to employ favorably the switch from ἐσθίων to τρώγων in the quotation of LXX Ps 41:9 in John 13:18. Though worthy of note, since it is intimately related to the issue of eucharistic imagery in the passage, the debate is not of great concern for the present study, as the study's interpretation of the passage is not dependent on the resolution of the issue, and the verb that describes the drinking of blood does not change. For more discussion, see Gignac, "Verbal Variety," 195.

13. Moloney, "When Is John Talking about Sacraments," 14.

14. Bultmann, *Das Evangelium des Johannes*, 98 (n. 2), 174, 525.

15. Cullmann, *Sacraments*. See also his subsequent work *Early Christian Worship*. For an analysis of the debate and the establishment of criteria by which one might judge the issue, see Brown, "Johannine Sacramentary Reconsidered," 183–206. See also his later *New Testament Essays*, 51–95. For a further development of Brown's criteria, see

which side of the debate one takes, it has been well established by many who have made a modern critical and comprehensive study of the Gospel that the words of John 6:53–56, whether original or a later ecclesiastical redaction, have a relationship in some degree to the eucharistic practice of the intended audience.[16]

Yet, even if one assumes this relationship, there is nevertheless much debate about the passage's primary purpose. Is it simply eucharistic, or is it christological?[17] Another category that may help discern the issue is Johannine eschatology. A significant and unique characteristic of the Fourth Gospel among the NT theologies is its realized eschatology (4:23; 5:25; 11:25).[18]

In John 6:40 this realized eschatology is enunciated by Jesus, "For this is the will of my Father, that everyone who sees (ὁ θεωρῶν) the Son and believes (πιστεύων) in him may have (ἔχῃ) eternal life, and I myself will raise (ἀναστήσω) him in the last day." The verbs in the first clauses are in the present tense, the verb in the last clause is in the future. The same construction appears in 6:54, "The one who eats (ὁ τρώγων) my flesh and drinks (πίνων) my blood has (ἔχει) eternal life, and I will raise (ἀναστήσω) him on the last day." Again, the verbs in the first clauses are all in the present tense, but the verb in the last clause is in the future. In summary, the one who eats and drinks now has eternal life, and that will be manifest in the future resurrection.

That the early Christians saw an eschatological aspect to the eucharistic gathering is indicated in other NT passages as well (1 Cor 11:26; Mark

---

Moloney, "When Is John Talking about Sacraments," 10–33; and Barrett, *Essays on John*, 37–97.

16. See, for example, Bernard, *Gospel According to St. John*, 1. 212; Hoskyns, *Fourth Gospel*, 304; Lightfoot, *St. John's Gospel*, 162; Bultmann, *Das Evangelium des Johannes*, 174; Barrett, *Gospel According to St. John*, 297; Dodd, *Interpretation of the Fourth Gospel*, 338; Schnackenburg, *Das Johannesevangelium*, 2.85. Brown, *Gospel According to John*, 1.284–85; Brodie, *Gospel According to John*, 286; Moloney, *Gospel of John*, 223–24; Culpepper, *Gospel and Letters of John*, 163; Keener, *Gospel of John*, 1.689–91; Lincoln, *Gospel According to Saint John*, 232–35; Neyrey, *Gospel of John*, 127. Some who have made a study of NT eucharistic imagery have also concluded likewise. See especially Jeremias, *Eucharistic Words*, 107; Kilpatrick, *Eucharist*, 55; and Kodell, *Eucharist*, 121–26.

17. For a summary of the debate, see Menken, "John 6:51c-58," 183–204. Hoskyns, however, doubted whether such distinctions would have been known to the author (*Fourth Gospel*, 304).

18. Matera, *New Testament Theology*, 311–14.

14:25; Luke 22:18).[19] The relevance of this for the present study is stated by Moloney: "Often in Johannine sacramental material, the author is concerned to show the reader, now distant from the events in the story, that she or he is still part of the story."[20] Thus, for the audience of the Fourth Gospel,

> The Eucharist is the way in which believers appropriate Jesus, the bread of life that has come down from heaven. When they believe in him as the bread that has come down from heaven and eat his flesh and drink his blood in the Eucharist, they have life in themselves and the promise of future resurrection life.[21]

In the eucharistic celebration the believer is united with Jesus who is united with the Father, and since the Father has life and Jesus has life because of the Father, the Christian has life because of Jesus (6:56; 10:38; 14:10–11).[22]

The Son of Man

The second indication that the author intended to direct attention to the death of Jesus is in another eschatological emphasis in 6:53, as the flesh and blood to be consumed is said to be that of the Son of Man. Elsewhere in the NT (Matt 24:30; 26:64; Mark 13:26; 14:62; Luke 21:27) and even in other Johannine literature (Rev 1:7; 14:14) this christological title is used to describe Jesus as the fulfillment of the figure coming on the clouds in the eschatological vision of Daniel (Dan 7:13). In this Gospel, however, the title points primarily to the crucifixion, death, and resurrection of Jesus.[23]

Though there are a number of indications of this emphasis in the Gospel, it is most clearly demonstrated in the three passages that refer to Jesus being "lifted up"—language that points to the cross (3:14–15; 8:28; 12:32–34).[24] All three of these passages employ the title "Son of Man." That

---

19. Brown, *Gospel According to John*, 1. 292.
20. Moloney, "Prolepsis," 133.
21. Matera, *New Testament Theology*, 310.
22. Schnackenburg, *Das Johannesevangelium*, 2. 94–95.
23. For the association of this title with the death of Jesus in this Gospel and specifically in its use in this discourse on the bread of life, see Moloney, *Son of Man*, 107–23. For a more recent discussion, see Matera, *New Testament Christology*, 232–34. For structural arguments relating the present passage to the crucifixion, see Girard, "Composition structurelle," 315–24; and Grassi, "John 6:51–58," 24–30.
24. Matera, *New Testament Christology*, 233.

Blood in the Gospel Preceding John 19:34

this same emphasis is intended in the bread of life discourse is indicated by the context of the subsequent occurrence of this title in the discourse: "Then what if you were to see the Son of Man going up to where he was before?" (6:62)—language that points again to the death and resurrection of Jesus.

Blood

A third indication in the present passage that it is intended to direct attention to the death of Jesus is specifically the mention of his blood. As discussed in the previous chapter of this study, the ancient world understood a loss of blood to be a loss of life. When enough of it was spilled there was death. The relationship is seen elsewhere in the NT (Matt 23:30, 35; 27:4, 6, 8; 27:24, 25; Luke 11:50, 51; 13:1; Acts 1:19; 5:28; 18:6; 20:26; 22:20; Rom 3:15; Rev 6:10; 16:3, 6; 17:6; 18:24; 19:2). That at least this basic association was intended by the author is indicated by the fact that the next and only other reference to Jesus' blood in the Gospel is when it is described as coming forth from his body after death (19:34).

Furthermore, as discussed in the previous chapter of this study, there are a number of passages in the NT that compare Jesus to a Passover lamb (1 Cor 5:7; 1 Pet 1:19) or sacrificial animal (Rom 3:24–25; 1 Cor 10:16–18; Eph 1:7) whose death and blood, through purification for sin, gave life to the world. The frequent occurrence of such metaphors indicates that this was part of the common parlance in the Christian cultural milieu of the intended audience of the Gospel. In some of these passages, as in the present, the image of blood is even paired with flesh, and there it is explicitly associated with Jesus' death on the cross (Eph 2:13–14; Col 1:20–22).[25]

CONCLUSION

There are two passages in the Gospel preceding 19:34 that contain references to blood. The first appears in the prologue where, based upon the cultural association of blood with life, it was used to describe a natural birth (1:13). The second reference to blood was in the discourse on the bread of life where the word "blood" was used in reference to the life-giving blood of Jesus (6:53–56). There are some indications in the passage (e.g., eucharistic

---

25. Menken, "John 5:51c–58," 190–91.

imagery, the reference to the Son of Man, and the very mention of blood itself) that this reference to life-giving blood was intended to direct attention to the death of Jesus.

As discussed in the previous chapter of this study, the intended audience of the Gospel would have already understood the death of Jesus to be life-giving. But the author's unique explanation and contribution to this idea appears at the end of the Gospel (19:34). In that context blood is no longer paired with flesh but with water. Chapter 4 of this study, therefore, examines the occurrences of water that appear before 19:34 in order to assist in the evaluation of this climactic event, in which water follows and flows together with the blood that came out of the side of Jesus' dead body.

4

Water in the Gospel Preceding John 19:34

INTRODUCTION

THE WORD "WATER" (ὕδωρ) appears quite frequently in the Fourth Gospel (1:26, 31, 33; 2:7, 9; 3:5, 23; 4:7, 10, 11, 13, 14, 15, 46; 5:7; 7:38; 13:5; 19:34) and its symbolism has been treated in a number of studies in recent decades.[1] As discussed in chapter 2 of this study, though drinking and washing with water are part of the daily routine of people everywhere, it was especially significant in the cultural milieu of the Fourth Gospel where the combination of arid climate, agrarian society, and cultic influences elevated its value and enabled it to convey a significant degree of religious symbolism. Water's natural cleansing property was used for its symbolic value in ritual purification, and water's use as an essential drink of life was used as a symbol for the life-giving power of the Spirit. These two general categories, purification and life, were evidently influential on the Gospel's water symbolism since, as will be seen, each symbolic occurrence of water imagery in the Gospel tends to fall neatly into one or the other of these same two categories. The present chapter examines the occurrences of the word "wa-

---

1. See Sciberras, "Water in the Gospel of St. John"; Becerra, "l'eau dans le Quatrième Évangile"; Culpepper, *Anatomy*, 192–95; Kowalski, "Of Water and Spirit"; Jones, *Symbol of Water in John*; Ng, *Water Symbolism in John*; Koester, *Symbolism in the Fourth Gospel*, 175–206.

41

ter" in the Gospel preceding 19:34 and demonstrates how these categories of water symbolism from the cultural environment are employed.[2]

RITUAL PURIFICATION AND JOHN'S BAPTISM WITH WATER (1:26, 31, 33)

Following the prologue, the Gospel tells a story about a delegation from Jerusalem sent by the Jews to inquire about John and his baptism (1:19–30). In John's answer to this delegation and subsequent monologue the following day, water appears three times:

1:26 ἀπεκρίθη αὐτοῖς ὁ Ἰωάννης λέγων· ἐγὼ βαπτίζω ἐν ὕδατι· μέσος ὑμῶν ἕστηκεν ὃν ὑμεῖς οὐκ οἴδατε.

John answered them, "I baptize with water, but among you stands one whom you do not know."

1:31 κἀγὼ οὐκ ᾔδειν αὐτόν, ἀλλ᾽ ἵνα φανερωθῇ τῷ Ἰσραὴλ διὰ τοῦτο ἦλθον ἐγὼ ἐν ὕδατι βαπτίζων.

I did not know him, but I came baptizing with water that he might be revealed to Israel.

1:33 κἀγὼ οὐκ ᾔδειν αὐτόν, ἀλλ᾽ ὁ πέμψας με βαπτίζειν ἐν ὕδατι ἐκεῖνός μοι εἶπεν· ἐφ᾽ ὃν ἂν ἴδῃς τὸ πνεῦμα καταβαῖνον καὶ μένον ἐπ᾽ αὐτόν, οὗτός ἐστιν ὁ βαπτίζων ἐν πνεύματι ἁγίῳ.

I did not know him, but the one who sent me to baptize with water said to me, "Upon whomever you see the Spirit descending and remaining is the one who baptizes with the Holy Spirit."

Water first appears in the Gospel, therefore, as the basic instrument of John's baptism. The verb βαπτίζειν has a wide range of meaning in Koine Greek but is employed in the NT to convey an action of ritual washing, whether literal or symbolic.[3]

---

2. The sea stories (John 6:16–25; 21:1–7) are not treated in the present study since these stories do not include the word "water" (ὕδωρ) and there does not appear to be a clear relationship of these stories with water symbolism in the Gospel. For a discussion of the symbolism of the sea in the Gospel, see Koester, *Symbolism in the Fourth Gospel*, 97–99, 134–36.

3. BDAG, s.v.

Water in the Gospel Preceding John 19:34

As discussed in chapter 2 of this study, in the cultural milieu of the Gospel, baptismal rites were commonly associated with ritual purification from uncleanness.[4] A prime example of this association is the baptismal rite of the community behind the DSS that called its initiatory baptismal rite "water of purification" (lit., "water of impurity" [מי נדה]1QS 3.3–5; 4.20–21; 5.13–14).[5] John's baptism, which may have been related to this rite,[6] was understood by Josephus in association with ritual purification as well (*A.J.* 18.5.2 §116–18; see also John 3:25).[7]

The Scriptures of Israel spoke often of a washing with water as a metaphor for spiritual cleansing (Ps 51:7; Isa 4:4; Jer 33:8) and even its association with an eschatological purification by the Spirit (Ezek 36:25–26; see also 1QS 4:20–21). The audience of the Gospel also knew of Christian baptism, which was associated early in the kerygma with the Spirit and purification as well (1 Cor 12:12–13; Titus 3:5). There was therefore within the cultural world of the Gospel a wealth of symbolism related to baptismal rites and their relationship with water's purificatory character and even associations of this character with the eschatological images of purification by the Spirit. Thus, while water is at first presented clearly as the mechanism of John's baptism, given the cultural context of the Gospel the author may have also expected the audience to see something more concerning the water mentioned in this passage.

This instance of water has been called the fountainhead that "sets the stage for subsequent use of water symbolism."[8] If the author intended the

---

4. For more discussion, see Hartman, "Baptism."

5. For a photographic reproduction and transliteration, see Burrows, Trever, and Brownlee, *Dead Sea Scrolls*. For the translation of the words מי נדה in the Rule of the Community, see Wernberg-Møller, *Manual of Discipline*, 24, 60. There also appears to have been a purificatory baptismal rite for the initiation of proselytes into contemporary Jewish sects and there may have been some relationship between this proselyte ritual and the baptism of John (Smith, "Jewish Proselyte Baptism," 25), but it is difficult to prove with certainty that Jewish proselyte baptism existed in the first century C.E.

6. Fitzmyer, *Dead Sea Scrolls and Christian Origins*, 18–21. For the significance of the DDS for Johannine studies, see Fitzmyer, "Qumran Literature and the Johannine Writings," 117–33.

7. Even though the author's primary portrayal of John is that of a witness more than a baptizer (Collins, "Johannine Characters," 362), his baptism is an integral part of this portrayal as it is mentioned a number of times in the Gospel (1:25, 26, 28, 31, 33; 3:23; 10:40) and is described as the instrument by which John recognized Jesus and was therefore enabled to witness to him.

8. Ng, *Water Symbolism in John*, 66–67.

audience to perceive a relationship between the roles of John and Jesus, then a similar relationship may have been intended between baptism with water and baptism with the Holy Spirit. As has been noted in a previous study:

> If water baptism symbolizes salvific cleansing brought about by the eschatological Christ, this symbolism works in an eschatological framework, in which the symbol prepares or anticipates the symbolized. Just as John the Baptist prepared the way for the eschatological Christ (2:23), his baptism anticipates salvific cleansing of the eschatological kingdom. So water anticipates the eschatological means of purification, which the gospel eventually comes to reveal as the Holy Spirit (7:37–39).[9]

Though this relationship may be subtle in the present passage, this does not negate the possibility that it was intended. As has been noted, "The reader cannot understand any part of the Fourth Gospel until he understands the whole."[10] If the author intended to imply a relationship between water and the Holy Spirit here, then that relationship should become more evident later in the Gospel, and it does (3:5; 7:38–39).[11]

In summary, water is first associated in the Gospel with the baptism of John. It is reasonable to assume from the cultural milieu of the Fourth Gospel that the author expected the audience to have some idea of a relationship between John's water baptism and ritual purification. Therefore, the first association of water in the Gospel falls into the category of purification. However, since this purification with water by John was said to be that which reveals the one who will baptize with the Holy Spirit, the author may be subtly hinting at a relationship between purification by water and purification by the Spirit.[12]

WATER IN JARS FOR JEWISH RITUALS OF PURIFICATION (2:7–9)

The second occurrence of water in the Gospel is in the story about a wedding at Cana (2:1–11). After a few details of the setting, the narrative

---

9. Ibid., 68.
10. Meeks, "Man from Heaven," 68.
11. Jones, *Symbol of Water in John*, 51.
12. Koester, *Symbolism in the Fourth Gospel*, 181.

Water in the Gospel Preceding John 19:34

quickly moves to the dialogue between Jesus and his mother (2:3–4). The wedding feast has run out of wine. The brevity of the exchange and the concise instructions of Jesus' mother to the servants help to convey the gravity of the problem.[13] In the midst of the crisis, Jesus is asked to do something, and the audience is confronted with his response, "My hour has not yet come" (2:4).[14]

The words beg for reflection. To which hour is Jesus referring? If the audience of the Gospel has any background in the oral Johannine tradition and if the theme of "the hour" existed in that tradition as it does in the written Gospel (2:4; 4:21, 23; 5:25, 28; 7:30; 8:20; 12:23, 27; 13:1; 17:1; 19:27), one would expect them to contemplate the coming passion where Jesus will explain that his hour has finally come (12:23; 17:24). If, however, the audience has had no earlier contact with the Johannine tradition, either oral or written, there is still in these words a direction of attention to a future time, which for a first-century Christian audience might point likewise to the passion.[15]

The narrator continues the story by informing the audience that in the vicinity were six stone jars for Jewish rituals of purification, each with a capacity of about 20–30 gallons (2:6).[16] In the narrator's description of what Jesus did with these jars, the word "water" appears twice:

2:7 λέγει αὐτοῖς ὁ Ἰησοῦς· γεμίσατε τὰς ὑδρίας ὕδατος. καὶ ἐγέμισαν αὐτὰς ἕως ἄνω.

Jesus said to them, "Fill the jars with water." And they filled them up to the brim.

2:8 καὶ λέγει αὐτοῖς· ἀντλήσατε νῦν καὶ φέρετε τῷ ἀρχιτρικλίνῳ· οἱ δὲ ἤνεγκαν.

Then he said to them, "Now draw some out and take it to the chief steward." So they took it.

---

13. Wine was an essential component of a first-century Jewish wedding feast, and the cultural implication of a shortage would have been significant (Derrett, "Water into Wine," 80–97; and more recently Williams, "Mother of Jesus at Cana," 679–92.

14. For a recent study concerning the idiom in the first part of Jesus' response, see Miller, "τί ἐμοὶ καὶ σοί."

15. For more discussion of the use of the term "hour" in the Fourth Gospel and the early kerygma in general, see Brown, *Gospel According to John*, 1.517–18.

16. For the volume of the Greek μετρητής, see BDAG, s.v.

> 2:9 ὡς δὲ ἐγεύσατο ὁ ἀρχιτρίκλινος τὸ ὕδωρ οἶνον γεγενημένον καὶ οὐκ ᾔδει πόθεν ἐστίν, οἱ δὲ διάκονοι ᾔδεισαν οἱ ἠντληκότες τὸ ὕδωρ, φωνεῖ τὸν νυμφίον ὁ ἀρχιτρίκλινος
>
> When the chief steward tasted the water which had become wine, and did not know from where it came (though the servants who had drawn the water knew), the chief steward called the bridegroom.

As in the previously examined passage concerning the baptism of John, here too water is associated with ritual purification since the water was put into jars designated for that purpose (2:6).[17] Yet, just as with the narrative detailing the image of water in John's baptism where attention was quickly redirected toward the baptism of the Spirit, here too in the present story attention is redirected, as the water in jars intended for ritual purification was transformed into something eminently drinkable, namely "good wine" (2:10).[18]

Being the common table beverage of the Mediterranean region of the Greco-Roman empire, wine played an integral part in the cultural context of the Gospel (Pliny, *Nat.* 14.6.53–14.22.118).[19] Among its many religious uses, wine was most significant in the Greek cult of Dionysius, the fertility god of vegetation in general and specifically of the vine. Because of the apparent similarities, Rudolf Bultmann suggested Dionysiac miracle stories as the background for the Cana story.[20] The primary cultural influence behind the Gospel, however, is not pagan legends and literature but rather first-century Judaism and the Scriptures of Israel. As such it is there that one should look for the background of the Cana sign:

> Jn. 2:1–12 must be studied in the light of its Old Testament background which provides the key to the symbolism of the passage. As the significance of its biblical background is more

---

17. For a discussion concerning the type of purification rites that would have employed jars such as these, see Keener, *Divine Purity*, 140–43. The detail that the jars were made of stone is probably due to purification requirements as well (Lev 11:33). For more discussion of this latter point, see Magen, "Purity in Second Temple Times," 46–52.

18. Heil, *Blood and Water*, 108. For a study of wine grades in the ancient world and what would have been understood to be "good wine" by the intended audience, see Stanley, "Wines in the Greek and Roman Worlds," 105–14.

19. For a study of the primary sources documenting wine usage in the Greek and Roman culture of the period, see Ferguson, "Wine as Table-Drink," 141–53.

20. Bultmann, *Das Evangelium des Johannes*, 83, 165; and more recently, Hengel, "Wine Miracle at Cana," 112.

Water in the Gospel Preceding John 19:34

firmly emphasized, Bultmann's theory that the essential motif of the story is borrowed from the Dionysius legend is proportionately relativized.[21]

In the Scriptures of Israel wine is described as a staple of daily life (Deut 8:8; 11:14). Its presence was a sign of prosperity (Gen 49:11–12; Prov 3:10), and an abundance of wine came to symbolize God's eschatological blessings (Isa 25:6; Jer 31:12; Amos 9:14; Joel 2:19; Zech 9:17).[22] Given this background, the audience would have interpreted the sign of wine in Cana as a demonstration that in Jesus the blessings of the messianic era had arrived.[23]

There are some details in the narrative, however, that indicate that the present access to these blessings is to be understood as fully dependent on a future event. The narrative refers to the "hour" which, as already discussed, directs the audience's attention to the coming passion, death, and resurrection of Jesus. This theme of the hour resurfaces in the words of the chief steward, when it is stated that the good wine has been saved until "now" (2:10). Just as "the hour" is an important theme running through the Gospel, so is the present access to that hour (4:23; 5:25; 11:25).[24] In the words of Francis J. Moloney, "The tension between the 'not yet' of the hour of Jesus (2:4) and the 'now' of the miracle story (2:10) is present in the narrator's comment that in this, the beginning of his signs (v. 11: *archē tōn sēmeiōn*), the *doxa* of Jesus was manifested."[25] At the Wedding in Cana, therefore, the future "hour" and its eschatological significance, though "not yet," is shown

---

21. Collins, "Cana," 81. See also Schnackenburg, *Das Johannesevangelium*, 1. 343–44. For linguistic arguments indicating that the LXX and not pagan literature was the primary literary influence on the Gospel, see Kilpatrick, "Religious Background of the Fourth Gospel," 36–44.

22. For a brief summary, see Sesboüé, "Vin," 1114–16. For the popularity of viticulture in Israel compared to that of its surrounding neighbors, see Matthews, "Treading the Winepress," 19–32. For a study of the major components of the typical meal in Israel and the place of wine, see Borowski, "Mediterranean Diet," 96–107. For more discussion concerning wine symbolism in ancient Israel and later Judaism, see Goodenough, *Jewish Symbols*, 5.100–111, 6.128–34.

23. Collins, "Cana," 88. The amount of wine that would have been created is difficult to imagine, as wine is not usually pictured today in quantities such as this. A more helpful image has been given by Collins who approximates the quantity as "640 to 940 bottles of wine" (ibid., 80).

24. For a study of this phenomenon, see Allison, *Passion and Resurrection of Jesus*, and Keener, *Gospel of John*, 1.501.

25. Moloney, *Gospel of John*, 69.

to be presently accessible, as the good wine was indeed served "now" (2:10) and the "glory" of Jesus began to be revealed (2:11).

In summary, it appears that the author expected the water in the wedding at Cana story to be associated first with ritual purification as the jars into which it was put were declared to have been designated for that purpose. But as in the story of John's baptism where water for ritual purification subsequently became the medium of revelation, a similar function is at play here. Water in jars reserved for ritual purification became something eminently drinkable, namely, good wine. Like the water of John's baptism, the water in the jars was used to reveal something about Jesus and his relationship to the eschatological hopes of Israel, specifically, that in him the blessings of the messianic era had arrived. The author shows, however, that while these blessings may be accessible "now," they are intimately dependent upon the events that will take place in the future "hour," when the "glory" that Jesus began to reveal at Cana will be fully manifest in his glorification on the cross.[26]

A NEW BIRTH AND PURIFICATION BY WATER AND THE SPIRIT (3:5)

The next appearance of the word "water" in the Gospel is in the dialogue with Nicodemus the Pharisee (3:1–15). Nicodemus opened the dialogue by stating his knowledge of Jesus' origin (3:2). Jesus responded with the words, "Amen, amen I say to you, no one can see the kingdom of God without being born anew (ἄνωθεν)" (3:3). Nicodemus was confused about the nature of this new birth (3:4). The adverb ἄνωθεν can mean either "from above" or "again,"[27] and Nicodemus is shown to have understood the latter in his response.[28] This led Jesus to elaborate, and it is here that the word "water" appears in the story:

---

26. For more discussion of the association of the Cana sign with the future "hour," see Heil, *Blood and Water*, 108; and the extensive study by Little, *Wine of Cana*.

27. BDAG, s.v. ἄνωθεν.

28. For a discussion of the literary technique of misunderstanding in the Gospel, see Brown, *Gospel According to John*, cxxxv–cxxxvi.

3:5 ἀπεκρίθη Ἰησοῦς· ἀμὴν ἀμὴν λέγω σοι, ἐὰν μή τις γεννηθῇ ἐξ ὕδατος καὶ πνεύματος, οὐ δύναται εἰσελθεῖν εἰς τὴν βασιλείαν τοῦ θεοῦ.

Jesus answered, "Amen, amen I say to you, unless one is born of water and the Spirit, he cannot enter the kingdom of God."

The audience has already heard about a potential relationship between water and the Spirit in the narrative about the baptism of John (1:26, 31, 33). When water and the Spirit are mentioned again, the author would anticipate a recollection of this former passage about baptism with water and baptism with the Spirit. The Christian audience of the Gospel would also be expected to know the relationship of water baptism and the Spirit, as this appears to have been an element of the early kerygma (1 Cor 12:12–13; Titus 3:5).[29] Finally, the language of a new birth in association with either water or the Spirit should recall for the audience baptismal imagery as well, since new birth imagery was one of the early Christian metaphors for baptism (Titus 3:5; 1 Pet 1:3).

In summary, in the dialogue with Nicodemus water is explicitly associated with the Spirit. Though there may be some questions concerning the specific details and referent of this relationship, it is highly probable given the preceding narrative and the cultural backdrop of the Gospel that this description of a new birth by water and the Spirit was intended to be associated with some sort of ritual purification, and probably a rite of baptism.[30] In the next occurrence of water the issue of purification appears again, where the baptisms of John and Jesus are set in tension.

JOHN'S BAPTISM, RITUAL PURIFICATION, AND THE WATER AT AENON (3:23)

Shortly after the Nicodemus narrative the Gospel tells of a conflict caused by a chronological overlapping of the ministries of Jesus and John. Jesus went into the land of Judea with his disciples and was baptizing (3:22). John is described as having continued to baptize elsewhere and it is in this detail that the word "water" appears:

29. Schnackenburg, *Das Johannesevangelium*, 1.383. As declared by Jones, "A reader familiar with Christian tradition would have difficulty not finding references to the practice of baptism throughout the passage" (*Symbolism of Water in John*, 75).

30. Burge, *Holy Spirit in the Johannine Tradition*, 166–67.

Seeing Blood and Water

> 3:23 Ἦν δὲ καὶ ὁ Ἰωάννης βαπτίζων ἐν Αἰνὼν ἐγγὺς τοῦ Σαλείμ, ὅτι ὕδατα πολλὰ ἦν ἐκεῖ, καὶ παρεγίνοντο καὶ ἐβαπτίζοντο·
>
> John was baptizing at Aenon, near Salim, because of the abundance of water there, and people were coming and being baptized.

The narrative goes on to describe a debate between John's disciples and a Jew over "purification" (3:25). When the disciples came to John, apparently for clarification on the issue, they declared that Jesus was baptizing and all were going to him (3:26).

Since water is described only as the mechanism of John's baptism the passage does not appear to expand the symbolism of water beyond that found in the previously examined occurrences.[31] As already discussed, John's baptism was associated with ritual purification. Whatever Jesus and his disciples were doing, their baptizing would have been in some way associated with this concept as well.[32] The mention of the debate between John's disciples and a "Jew" about "purification" reinforces the significance of the purification theme[33] and may have been intended to recall for the audience when the "Jews" sent to inquire about John and his baptism earlier in the Gospel (1:19).

DRINKING LIVING WATER WITHOUT A BUCKET (4:7–15)

The next occurrence of the word "water" is in the story about a dialogue between Jesus and a Samaritan woman. The narrative is set at a well in Samaria around the noon hour (4:5–6). Jesus was tired and sat down near the well (4:6). When a woman approached, a dialogue ensued and it is here that the word "water" makes a number of appearances:

> 4:7 ἔρχεται γυνὴ ἐκ τῆς Σαμαρείας ἀντλῆσαι ὕδωρ. λέγει αὐτῇ ὁ Ἰησοῦς· δός μοι πεῖν·
>
> A woman of Samaria came to draw water. Jesus said to her, "Give me a drink."
>
> 4:8 οἱ γὰρ μαθηταὶ αὐτοῦ ἀπεληλύθεισαν εἰς τὴν πόλιν ἵνα τροφὰς ἀγοράσωσιν.

---

31. Jones, *Symbol of Water in John*, 85.
32. Burge, *Holy Spirit in the Johannine Tradition*, 165.
33. Jones, *Symbol of Water in John*, 85. See also Keener, *Divine Purity*, 152.

(His disciples had gone into the city to buy food.)

4:9 λέγει οὖν αὐτῷ ἡ γυνὴ ἡ Σαμαρῖτις· πῶς σὺ Ἰουδαῖος ὢν παρ' ἐμοῦ πεῖν αἰτεῖς γυναικὸς Σαμαρίτιδος οὔσης; οὐ γὰρ συγχρῶνται Ἰουδαῖοι Σαμαρίταις.[34]

The Samaritan woman said to him, "How is it that you, a Jew, ask for a drink from me, a Samaritan woman?" (For Jews do not share things in common with Samaritans.)

4:10 ἀπεκρίθη Ἰησοῦς καὶ εἶπεν αὐτῇ· εἰ ᾔδεις τὴν δωρεὰν τοῦ θεοῦ καὶ τίς ἐστιν ὁ λέγων σοι· δός μοι πεῖν, σὺ ἂν ᾔτησας αὐτὸν καὶ ἔδωκεν ἄν σοι ὕδωρ ζῶν.

Jesus answered her, "If you knew the gift of God and who it is that is saying to you, 'Give me a drink,' you would have asked him and he would have given you living water."

4:11 λέγει αὐτῷ ἡ γυνή· κύριε, οὔτε ἄντλημα ἔχεις καὶ τὸ φρέαρ ἐστὶν βαθύ· πόθεν οὖν ἔχεις τὸ ὕδωρ τὸ ζῶν;[35]

The woman said to him, "Sir, you have no bucket and the cistern is deep. Where do you get this living water?"

4:12 μὴ σὺ μείζων εἶ τοῦ πατρὸς ἡμῶν Ἰακώβ, ὃς ἔδωκεν ἡμῖν τὸ φρέαρ καὶ αὐτὸς ἐξ αὐτοῦ ἔπιεν καὶ οἱ υἱοὶ αὐτοῦ καὶ τὰ θρέμματα αὐτοῦ;

"Are you greater than our ancestor Jacob who gave us the cistern and who, with his sons and flocks, drank from it?"

4:13 ἀπεκρίθη Ἰησοῦς καὶ εἶπεν αὐτῇ· πᾶς ὁ πίνων ἐκ τοῦ ὕδατος τούτου διψήσει πάλιν·

Jesus responded, "Whoever drinks this water will thirst again!"

---

34. The last clause in 4:9 (οὐ γὰρ συγχρῶνται Ἰουδαῖοι Σαμαρίταις) is lacking in the first hand of Sinaiticus, Bezae, a number of Old Latin witnesses, and the Fayyumic Coptic (NA[27]). However, given the clause's early and diversified attestation (P[63], P[66], P[75], P[76], and the rest of the manuscript tradition) it can be assumed to be original. The absence of the clause in the few witnesses listed above is most likely due to homoioteleuton with Σαμαρίτιδος and various subsequent scribal modifications (Kilpatrick, "John 4:9," 327-28).

35. In 4:11, NA[27] has brackets around the words ἡ γυνή. The present study has left them off in its presentation of the text since the variant is not exegetically relevant for the study and there is a strong likelihood that the words are authentic.

Seeing Blood and Water

4:14 ὃς δ' ἂν πίῃ ἐκ τοῦ ὕδατος οὗ ἐγὼ δώσω αὐτῷ, οὐ μὴ διψήσει εἰς τὸν αἰῶνα, ἀλλὰ τὸ ὕδωρ ὃ δώσω αὐτῷ γενήσεται ἐν αὐτῷ πηγὴ ὕδατος ἁλλομένου εἰς ζωὴν αἰώνιον.

"But whoever drinks the water that I will give will never thirst. The water that I will give will become in that person a well of water springing up to eternal life."

4:15 λέγει πρὸς αὐτὸν ἡ γυνή· κύριε, δός μοι τοῦτο τὸ ὕδωρ, ἵνα μὴ διψῶ μηδὲ διέρχωμαι ἐνθάδε ἀντλεῖν.

The woman said to him, "Sir, give me this water, so that I may not be thirsty or have to keep coming here to draw water."

The story continues with a discussion about the woman's marital history and ethnicity, and this leads to a series of developments about Jesus' identity. The story then concludes with the conversion of the nearby Samaritan city (4:16–42).

Jesus described the water that he would give as "living water" (4:10). As in the previous narrative with Nicodemus, there is a play on a naive misunderstanding since the phrase can be understood in two ways. At the most basic level, "living water" (ὕδωρ ζῶν) means moving water, as opposed to standing water.[36] Moving water is naturally preferred to standing water for drinking as it is ordinarily perceived to be fresher and cleaner. But, moving water was also required for ritual purification in the Mosaic Law common to Jews and Samaritans alike (Lev 14:5–6, 50–52; 15:13; Num 19:17).[37]

The dominant image of water in this passage, however, is based upon its natural use for drinking and sustaining life. This is indicated by the numerous references to drinking (4:7, 9, 10, 12, 13, 14), and the description of the living water as a spring inside a person that causes one never to thirst (4:14, 15). But the words of Jesus in this passage are not intended to refer to a miraculous internal source of water in the literal sense, though this is the understanding of the woman (4:15).[38]

---

36. See, for example, in both the MT (מַיִם חַיִּים) and the LXX (ὕδωρ ζῶν) Gen 26:19; Cant 4:15.

37. The purification theme observed in the previously examined occurrences of water may also be in the background here, and this may be further indicated by the narrator's explanation, "Jews do not share things in common with Samaritans (4:9)" (Keener, *Divine Purity*, 150–51).

38. See Brown on the literary technique of "Johannine misunderstanding" in this passage and the interchange of the Greek words πηγή and φρέαρ (*Gospel According to*

Rather, the words "living water" should remind the audience of an image that already occurred earlier in the Gospel, especially when in the present context Jesus refers to himself as the source. In the prophetic literature of Israel "living water" appears flowing from the eschatological temple (Zech 14:8; Joel 4:18; see also Ezek 47:1, 8-9).[39] The audience of the Gospel has already heard that Jesus is the temple of God (2:19-22; see also 1:14). Now Jesus is described as a source of living water like the eschatological temple in the prophetic literature of Israel. The temple theme resurfaces again later in the story when the woman asks for Jesus' position on the debate between the Jews and Samaritans regarding the proper place of worship (4:20).

In summary, water is first mentioned in the story of the Samaritan woman as a basic necessity of life since she is said to come to the well to draw water and Jesus asked for a drink. Water symbolism is developed in the passage when water is offered by Jesus to those who thirst as "living water." This mention of living water was likely intended to remind the audience of the same image in the prophetic literature of Israel where living water is said to flow from the eschatological temple in Jerusalem. Since Jesus was already identified as the temple of God earlier in the Gospel the author is showing that Jesus, as this new temple, is the fulfillment of the eschatological hopes of Israel.[40] He is the great temple of God seen by the prophets of Israel and, as such, is a source of life that, like water, flows from him to those who drink, "springing up to eternal life" (4:14).[41]

DRINKING LIVING WATER AND THE HOLY SPIRIT (7:37–39)

The next symbolic use of the word "water" in the Gospel is in the narrative describing Jesus' words during the festival of Booths.[42] The surrounding

---

John, 1. 170).

39. In Zechariah the water is said to flow from Jerusalem, but the other references to the temple elsewhere in the book, and the role of the temple in the festival of Booths mentioned in conjunction with this vision, indicates that "Jerusalem" in this context is a metonymic for the temple (Meyers and Meyers, *Zechariah 9–14*, 435–36).

40. Keener, *Divine Purity*, 154–55.

41. For more on temple imagery in the Gospel, see Coloe, *Temple Symbolism in the Fourth Gospel*.

42. There is one other earlier occurrence of the word "water" (5:7) and the story in which it occurs was understood in the patristic era to have baptismal symbolism. The

Seeing Blood and Water

narrative focuses on the debate about Jesus' identity. Some thought he was a good man, others thought he was deceiving the people, but as the narrator relates, "For fear of the Jews, no one spoke openly about him" (7:13). Water imagery appears when Jesus makes a dramatic public proclamation:

7:37 Ἐν δὲ τῇ ἐσχάτῃ ἡμέρᾳ τῇ μεγάλῃ τῆς ἑορτῆς εἱστήκει ὁ Ἰησοῦς καὶ ἔκραξεν λέγων· ἐάν τις διψᾷ ἐρχέσθω πρός με καὶ πινέτω. 7:38a ὁ πιστεύων εἰς ἐμέ,[43]

On the last and great day of the festival, Jesus stood up and cried out, "Let anyone who is thirsty come to me and the one who believes in me drink!"

7:38b καθὼς εἶπεν ἡ γραφή, ποταμοὶ ἐκ τῆς κοιλίας αὐτοῦ ῥεύσουσιν ὕδατος ζῶντος.

As the Scripture says, "Rivers of living water shall flow from his belly."

7:39 τοῦτο δὲ εἶπεν περὶ τοῦ πνεύματος ὃ ἔμελλον λαμβάνειν οἱ πιστεύσαντες εἰς αὐτόν· οὔπω γὰρ ἦν πνεῦμα, ὅτι Ἰησοῦς οὐδέπω ἐδοξάσθη.

He said this in reference to the Spirit that those who believe in him were to receive, there was no Spirit yet, because Jesus had not yet been glorified.

---

occurrence of the word "water" is only incidental to the story, however, as the invalid is healed directly by Jesus. This story, therefore, does not appear to relate to water symbolism in the Gospel (Culpepper, *Anatomy*, 194; see also Jones, *Symbol of Water in John*, 135–36, and Koester, *Symbolism in the Fourth Gospel*, 190–92). Ng treats the passage in her section titled, "Symbolic References That Are Uncertain" (pp. 61–62), but her explanation of the possible water symbolism in the passage is related less to water than to the story's overall role in the general structure of the Gospel (p. 62).

43. The punctuation of 7:37–38 has been the subject of much debate in recent decades (for a brief history of the debate, see Keener, *Gospel of John*, 1. 728–29). Is the text to be separated according to the traditional verse division (7:37, 38) or as above (7:37–38a, 38b)? With the separation according to the traditional verse division a definite ambiguity exists. Who is the referent for the possessive pronoun in 7:38b? When the division is made as above, the believer appears to be the more likely candidate. But ambiguity remains even with this division (Menken, *Old Testament Quotations in the Fourth Gospel*, 188). Fortunately the resolution of this punctuation problem is not required for the purpose of the present study since with either division the exegetical conclusions regarding water symbolism in the passage remain substantially the same. For stylistic arguments in favor of the punctuation division accepted in this study, see Kilpatrick, "John VII. 37–38," 340–42.

Water in the Gospel Preceding John 19:34

In the previous chapter of the Gospel, Jesus was compared to the manna that Israel ate in the wilderness (John 6:31–40, 49–51). The subsequent episode in Exodus describes how when Israel was thirsty for water God gave them water from a rock (Exod 17:1–17; Num 20:2–13; 21:16). With this sequence of events in Exodus it might be expected that the author of the Gospel, after having described Jesus in comparison to the manna, would then describe him as a source of water like the rock in the wilderness that gave water to those who were thirsty.[44] At least two details in the present narrative further support this conclusion.

First, the occasion of Jesus' words is the final day of the festival of Booths. The week-long festival took place in the fall and, though a simple harvest celebration in origin (Exod 23:16), it came to be understood as a commemoration of the forty-year wandering in the wilderness. This understanding is evident in the prescription of the festival in Leviticus: "You shall dwell in booths for seven days . . . so that your generation will know that I made the children of Israel dwell in booths when they went forth from Egypt" (Lev 23:42–43).[45] The rock supplied Israel with water when they went forth from Egypt (Exod 17:1–17) and during the wilderness wandering (Num 20:2–13; 21:16). The setting of Jesus' words in the midst of the feast of Booths would further emphasize for the audience the association of Jesus with the water-giving rock.

Second, some in the crowd who heard Jesus' words concluded that he was the prophet (John 7:40). This identification refers to the prediction of the advent of a prophet like Moses (Deut 18:15–18).[46] Since it was Moses who struck the rock to bring forth the water during Israel's wandering (Exod 17:1–6; Num 20:2–13), this identification of Jesus as the prophet like Moses in conjunction with Jesus' words offering water to those who thirsted offers further evidence that the author intended a comparison of Jesus, not only with Moses, but even with the water-giving rock itself.[47] Thus, at one level, the author is describing Jesus as the fulfillment of the role of the life-saving rock in the wilderness similar to the portrayal of Jesus as

---

44. Menken, *Old Testament Quotations in the Fourth Gospel*, 195. See also the similar use of the same imagery in 1 Cor 10:4.

45. For more discussion concerning the origins of the festival, see Maertens, *Feast in Honor of Yahweh*, 32–35, 62–97.

46. Bernard, *Gospel According to St. John*, 1. 285–86.

47. Menken, *Old Testament Quotations in the Fourth Gospel*, 195.

Seeing Blood and Water

the fulfillment of the role of the life-saving manna. Yet, there is more to the imagery of water in this passage.

Water is described here as "living water" (7:38b). This phrase combined with the invitation for those who thirst to come to him and drink (7:37) recalls the story of Jesus' dialogue with the Samaritan woman (4:10–11). Since both passages described Jesus as a source of sustenance for those who thirst, and both passages employ the phrase "living water" (4:10–11), the audience would likely see a relationship between the two stories.[48]

In the story about the dialogue with the Samaritan woman, Jesus was described as the eschatological temple out of which flows "living water" as seen in the prophetic literature of Israel (Zech 14:8; Joel 4:18; see also Ezek 47:1, 8–9). As could be expected, when the words "living water" appear again in the present story, the same temple symbolism resurfaces, and this is indicated by the setting of the festival of Booths.

By the first century an elaborate temple ceremony had developed in conjunction with the festival. For a whole week crowds of pilgrims gathered in the temple area to participate in a daily ritual that climaxed with a priest pouring water on the altar.[49] As already discussed, the festival had roots in the fall harvest celebrations and so this water ritual is probably related to a prayer for future rain.[50]

It was on the last day of the festival, after a week of this water-pouring ritual, that Jesus made his public proclamation and invitation to those who thirst (7:37). Thus Jesus' words draw attention to the polemical relationship between his identity as the eschatological temple of Israel's prophetic literature and the temple in Jerusalem. Though this polemic was already employed in the story about the cleansing of the temple (2:13–22) and the dialogue with the Samaritan woman (4:7–15), it is reinforced by the

---

48. Hodges, "Rivers of Living Water," 242–43.

49. There is a detailed account of the temple ritual and explanation of its meaning in the Mishnah (*m. Sukkah*) and Tosefta (*t. Sukkah*). It is impossible, however, to know the historical accuracy of the details and the date of the development of the explanation, and thus its relevancy for the Gospel story. The present study assumes here that at least some sort of simple water-pouring ceremony occurred during the festival in the first century. For an argument in favor of the historicity of the details in the Mishnah and Tosefta and their relationship to the present narrative, see Koester, *Symbolism in the Fourth Gospel*, 194–98; and Keener, *Divine Purity*, 157–60. For more discussion concerning the festival and specifically the water-pouring ceremony, see Maertens, *Feast in Honor of Yahweh*, 62–97.

50. For example, see Zech 14:17. For more discussion, see Maertens, *Feast in Honor of Yahweh*, 72–73.

Water in the Gospel Preceding John 19:34

repetition of the same imagery and the new setting of the present passage in the midst of the last "day" of the festival of Booths.

The reason is that while the image of the living water flowing from the eschatological temple was already employed in the dialogue with the Samaritan woman, the same chapter of Zechariah that mentions the "living water" not only describes it as flowing "on that day" (14:1, 8; 13:1) but also describes a great eschatological "festival of Booths," when people from all nations would gather in Jerusalem to worship the God of Israel as king (14:16).[51]

Beyond this reinforcement of water symbolism with the living water of the eschatological temple, the passage also contributes further to the Gospel's water symbolism by clarifying the relationship between water and the Holy Spirit. The relationship of water and the Spirit in the cultural context has already been discussed in chapter 2 of this study. The relationship has also already been observed in earlier occurrences of water imagery in the Gospel (1:33; 3:5). But what is new here is the explicit declaration that the "living water" that Jesus as the eschatological temple offers to those who thirst is the Spirit (7:39).

Another related conclusion can be made as well, since it is also stated explicitly that the Holy Spirit would be received by the believer and that this will happen once Jesus is glorified (7:39). Later in the Gospel Jesus promises that the Spirit would be in the disciples (14:15–17), and after the resurrection he is described as giving them the Spirit (20:21–23). The idea that the Christian is a temple of God with the indwelling Spirit is found elsewhere in the kerygma (1 Cor 3:16; 6:19–20; see also 1 Pet 2:5), but the Gospel's contribution to this kerygma, or at least clarification of it, is that the giving of the Spirit is intimately connected with the events surrounding the death and resurrection of Jesus which is his "glorification" in the Gospel.

In summary, given the larger narrative structure of the Gospel where the present passage follows that which described Jesus as the manna in the wilderness, it is likely that Jesus' invitation to those who thirst to come to him and drink was intended by the author as a comparison of Jesus to the water-giving rock in the wilderness. But since Jesus' words employ the phrase "living water," they were also intended to recall for the audience the eschatological temple imagery from Israel's prophetic literature already employed in the dialogue with the Samaritan woman. This imagery is

---

51. Jones, *Symbol of Water in John*, 160. See also Ng, *Water Symbolism in John*, 80; and Koester, *Symbolism in the Fourth Gospel*, 198.

reinforced here by the setting of the festival of Booths, which recalls for the audience the association of the living water flowing from the eschatological temple during the great eschatological festival of Booths described by the prophet Zechariah. Finally, the passage states explicitly that the "living water" that Jesus offers to those who thirst is the Spirit and that the believer who comes to Jesus will receive the Spirit once Jesus has been glorified. Thus the passage also makes clear that the one who believes in Jesus receives the Spirit as living water, but that this experience is directly dependent upon the death and resurrection of Jesus.

PURIFICATION OF THE DISCIPLES BY A WASHING WITH WATER (13:5)

The next occurrence of the word "water" in the Gospel is also the last appearance preceding 19:34.[52] The story begins with a reference to Jesus' premonition of his coming passion, death, and resurrection, and it then describes how this led to the washing of the disciples' feet (13:1-3).

> 13:5 εἶτα βάλλει ὕδωρ εἰς τὸν νιπτῆρα καὶ ἤρξατο νίπτειν τοὺς πόδας τῶν μαθητῶν καὶ ἐκμάσσειν τῷ λεντίῳ ᾧ ἦν διεζωσμένος.
>
> Then he poured water into the washbasin and began to wash the disciples' feet and dry them with the towel that was tied around his waist.

Though the word "water" appears only once in the narrative it is a significant detail, since the theme of washing pervades the whole (13:5, 6, 8a, 8b, 10, 12, 14a, 14b).[53] At the most basic level, water functions in the story as a mechanism of natural cleansing. In the *Sitz-im-Leben* of the biblical narratives, with the dusty roads and open sandals worn by those that walked along them, footwashing was a common part of daily life (Gen 18:4;

---

52. The healing of the young blind man (9:1-41), which intervenes between the story of Jesus' words at the festival of Booths and the washing of the disciples' feet, has been interpreted by some to relate to the symbolism of water in the Gospel. Since the word "water" does not occur in the narrative, however, and its relation to water symbolism is questionable, it is not treated in this study. For more discussion of the issue, see Jones, *Symbol of Water in John*, 174-76; Ng, *Water Symbolism in John*, 64-66; and Koester, *Symbolism in the Fourth Gospel*, 108-9, 200.

53. Jones, *Symbol of Water in John*, 195.

Water in the Gospel Preceding John 19:34

19:2; 24:32; 43:24; Judg 19:21; 1 Sam 25:41; 2 Sam 11:8; Luke 7:44; 1 Tim 5:10). That there is more to the episode, however, than a simple record of Jesus encouraging basic etiquette is indicated by the cultural connection of footwashing to ritual purification and the underlying theme of the Johannine narrative.

Ritual footwashing was commanded for the priests before entrance into the sanctuary (Exod 30:19). The context of this requirement in Exodus and Philo's explanations of the meaning of the passage suggest that footwashing would have been understood in the cultural context of the Gospel, not only in relation to basic etiquette, but ritual purification as well.[54]

The underlying theme of the Johannine footwashing narrative is first indicated when it is said that Jesus' premonition of his coming death led to the footwashing (13:1–3). At the end of the dialogue with Peter there is a reference to the coming betrayal.[55] The betrayal will lead to Jesus' death (13:10–11).[56] Thus the background theme of Jesus' coming death frames the washing episode and indicates that etiquette was not the intended focus of the story.[57] Rather, this background theme coupled with the cultural association of footwashing with ritual purification indicates that the washing of the disciples' feet symbolizes the spiritual purification the disciples will receive through the coming death of Jesus on the cross (13:10).[58]

The symbolism of water in this passage, therefore, is related once again to ritual purification.[59] The symbolism is based on the natural cleansing

---

54. For Philo's understanding of Exod 30:19 in relation to ritual purification, see especially *Mos.* 2.138; *Spec.* 1.206-7. For more discussion concerning the custom and its relationship to ritual purification in Judaism and the Christian kerygma, see Weiss, "Footwashing."

55. For the relationship of the betrayal and the footwashing, see Moloney, "John 13:1-38," 1-16.

56. There may also be a subtle hint to his coming death and resurrection in the laying aside of his garments and putting them on again (Hoskyns, *John*, 376; Brown, *Gospel According to John*, 2. 551). But this has been challenged (Schnackenburg, *Das Johannesevangelium*, 3. 19).

57. Culpepper, "*Hypodeigma*," 134-41.

58. Jones, *Symbol of Water in John*, 196. It is also possible, given the cultural function of footwashing as part of the reception of someone into the home, that this footwashing is a sign that Jesus' disciples are now being welcomed into the home of the Father and thus have become, as the prologue says, "children of God" (John 1:12). For more discussion, see Hultgren, "Johannine Footwashing," 539-46; and Coloe, "Foot Washing," 400-415. For more discussion concerning footwashing and John 13, see Thomas, *Footwashing*.

59. Ng, *Water Symbolism in John*, 81-83.

property of water, as in a customary footwashing in first-century Judea. This natural cleansing, along with the association of the custom with ritual purification, is used as a symbol of the spiritual cleansing that will come with the death of Jesus. Thus the passage anticipates a future cleansing in association with the death of Jesus as the previously examined passage anticipated a future gift of life through the Spirit after Jesus' glorification.

CONCLUSION

Chapter 2 of this study provided a preliminary examination of John 19:34, its surrounding pericope (19:31–37), and the cultural assumptions concerning the images of blood and water. Chapter 3 examined the occurrences of the word "blood" that precede 19:34 in the Gospel and demonstrated how the cultural assumptions concerning blood are employed. The present chapter has done likewise with respect to the preceding occurrences of the word "water." These preceding occurrences of water fell into two major categories based upon the two basic uses of water from the cultural context—cleansing and drinking for sustenance of life.

The natural characteristic of cleansing was used as a symbol in ritual purification and most importantly that which can only be accomplished by the power of the Spirit. This purification symbolism was employed in the occurrences of water in the stories about John's baptism (1:26, 31, 33; 3:23), the wedding at Cana (2:7, 9; 4:46), the dialogue with Nicodemus (3:5), and the washing of the disciples' feet (13:5).

The natural need for water as an essential drink for sustenance of life was used as a symbol of the life-giving power of the Spirit that, when imbibed by the believer, became an internal surging spring of living water, springing up to eternal life. This symbolism of drinking living water was employed in the occurrences of water in the dialogue with the Samaritan woman (4:7, 10, 11, 13, 14, 15), and Jesus' words at the festival of Booths (7:38).

These two major aspects of water symbolism, that of purification and life, and the association of both of these aspects with the Spirit will appear again in the last occurrence of the word "water" in the Gospel. There, however, water symbolism will not stand alone, as the word "water" occurs along with the word "blood" (19:34).

Chapter 5 of this study examines these final occurrences of the words "blood" and "water" and demonstrates how the author employs both the symbolism from the cultural setting and the development of this symbolism in the preceding Gospel narrative. In the context of these final occurrences the author declares that the scene fulfills a passage from the prophetic writings of Israel (19:37). In this dramatic declaration the author gives the audience all the remaining information they yet need to complete their understanding of the climactic event of blood and water flowing forth from the pierced side of Jesus' dead body (19:34).

5

The Interpretation of John 19:34

INTRODUCTION

CHAPTER 1 OF THE present study summarized the history of interpretation of John 19:34. Chapter 2 examined the manuscript tradition of this verse along with its immediate literary context (19:31–37) and supplied a summary of the symbolic significance of the images of blood and water in the cultural milieu of the Gospel. Chapters 3 and 4 then showed how this symbolic significance of blood and water influenced the manner in which the words "blood" and "water" were used in the Gospel preceding 19:34.

The present chapter completes this exegetical analysis with a focused examination of John 19:34 in its immediate literary context (19:31–37). In so doing, this chapter demonstrates how the symbolic significance from the cultural milieu that had influenced the use of the words "blood" and "water" in the Gospel preceding 19:34 influenced the use of these words again. The chapter then completes its analysis with an application of the study's findings to the question concerning the relationship of 19:34 to the sacramental life of the Gospel's intended audience.

THE PIERCING OF JESUS' SIDE AND THE FULFILLMENT OF SCRIPTURE (19:31–37)

The final appearance of the words "blood" and "water" in the Gospel occurs in the midst of a pericope describing the events immediately following

The Interpretation of John 19:34

Jesus' death and their relationship to the Scriptures of Israel (19:31–37).[1] The narrative begins with the chronological setting. It was the Preparation Day (19:31, see also 19:14), described as "particularly solemn" (μεγάλη) since preparations were being made for both the weekly Sabbath and the annual festival of Passover (Exod 12:16).[2]

The word "day" (ἡμέρα) is modified by this same adjective (μεγάλη) only one other time in the Gospel (7:37). Such a description of the day's significance in the present context, therefore, was probably intended not only to convey a sense of solemnity for the present setting, but also to remind the audience of that earlier narrative when Jesus on the "great" (μεγάλη) day of the festival of Booths invited those who were thirsty to come to him and drink (7:37–39).[3] The audience is also reminded, therefore, of the narrator's explanation that the "living water" mentioned by Jesus was a metaphor for the Spirit that would be available only after Jesus had been glorified (7:39). Jesus' glorification has now begun and thus the recollection of this earlier prediction alerts the audience to the imminence of its fulfillment.[4]

Following the details of the setting, the audience is told that the Jews requested that the legs of those who were crucified be broken and that their bodies be taken away (19:31). Left alone, crucified individuals could survive for several days. The breaking of their legs could significantly shorten this survival period, however, by hastening the onset of suffocation.[5] This request by the Jews is said to have been motivated by a concern that the bodies not remain on the cross during the Sabbath (19:31); it was forbidden by Mosaic Law for a body to remain hanging on a tree after sunset (Deut 21:22–23; see also Josh 8:29).[6] However, the detail about this request by the

---

1. For a presentation of the Greek text of the pericope (19:31–37), see chapter 2 of this study.

2. Bernard, *Gospel According to St. John*, 2.623, 642–43.

3. Schnackenburg, *Das Johannesevangelium*, 3.334.

4. As is discussed below, the death of Jesus is actually part of a larger process of glorification that results in the gift of the Spirit (John 20:19–23). The point was summarized well by Brown when he said that the gift of the Spirit "flows from the whole process of glorification in 'the hour' of the passion, death, resurrection, and ascension" (*Gospel According to John*, 2. 951). See also Burge, *Holy Spirit in the Johannine Tradition*, 133–35. For a discussion concerning the uniqueness of the Johannine glorification theme among the NT theologies, see Matera, *New Testament Theology*, 314–16.

5. For more discussion, see Keener, *Gospel of John*, 2.1150.

6. That this law was applied to crucifixion in the first century is indicated not only by the present passage but by Josephus as well who states that the Jews were careful to bury before sunset those who had been crucified (*B.J.* 4.5.2 §317). See also the reference

Seeing Blood and Water

Jews is probably intended to convey more than a simple historical factor for the events that follow. Irony is one of the favorite literary techniques employed in this Gospel, and there is obvious irony in this concern to keep a statute of the Mosaic Law by those who had wrongfully accused and handed over Jesus for crucifixion and, contrary to the Mosaic Law, proclaimed a foreigner as their king (John 19:15; Deut 17:15).[7]

In response to the request soldiers came and broke the legs of the two individuals who had been crucified with Jesus (19:32), but seeing that Jesus was already dead they did not break his legs (19:33). In the description of what the soldiers did next the words "blood" and "water" make their final appearance in the Gospel.

> 19:34 ἀλλ' εἷς τῶν στρατιωτῶν λόγχῃ αὐτοῦ τὴν πλευρὰν ἔνυξεν, καὶ ἐξῆλθεν εὐθὺς αἷμα καὶ ὕδωρ.
>
> Instead, one of the soldiers stabbed his side with a spear, and immediately there came out blood and water.

The narrative progression of the pericope pauses at this moment as the narrator addresses the audience directly, testifying to the reliability of this information and its relevance for the audience's belief (19:35).[8] The relevance is further emphasized by the declaration that the events just narrated fulfilled two passages of Scripture.

The fact that the soldiers did not break the legs of Jesus is said to fulfill a Scripture passage that states, "None of his bones will be crushed" (19:36). Two images from the Scriptures of Israel immediately present themselves as possibly intended referents. One is the Passover lamb; it was prohibited to break even one of its bones (Exod 12:46; Num 9:12; see also LXX Exod 12:10). The other is the "just man" described in Psalm 34; it is said that God watches over him, even his bones, so that "not one of them will be broken" (34:20; LXX Ps 33:21). Both of these images are equally plausible referents, and given the Passover setting of the story and the wrongful execution of

---

to Deut 21:22–23 in Gal 3:13 and similar imagery in Acts 5:30; 10:39; 13:29; 1 Pet 2:24.

7. Concerning the use of irony in 19:31, see Moloney, *Gospel of John*, 505; Keener, *Gospel of John*, 2.1151; and Neyrey, *Gospel of John*, 313. For a discussion about the various literary techniques employed in the Gospel, see Brown, *Gospel According to John*, cxxxv–cxxxvi.

8. For more discussion concerning the significance of this verse for the Gospel as a whole and the similar statement in 21:24, see chapter 1 of this study and Brown, *Introduction to the Gospel of John*, 152, 182–83.

The Interpretation of John 19:34

Jesus the just man (John 18:18; 19:4, 6), it is altogether likely that the author of the Gospel intended both images to be understood as being fulfilled together in the present narrative.[9]

The second event in the story—the soldier stabbing Jesus' side (19:34)—is declared by the narrator to fulfill a Scripture passage as well (19:37a). The passage is quoted as "They shall look at him whom they have pierced" (19:37b). The intended referent is undoubtedly Zech 12:10.[10] After this last citation the narrative progression of the Gospel continues again, now with the story detailing the burial of Jesus' body by Joseph of Arimathea and Nicodemus (19:38–42).

BLOOD IN THE CULTURE AND GOSPEL PRECEDING 19:34

As discussed in chapter 2 of this study, there were certain cultural presuppositions that the intended audience would recall when hearing about blood coming forth from the side of Jesus' body in John 19:34. In summary, the Scriptures of Israel describe blood as the seat of life and based upon this concept blood was used for the ritual purification of sin in Israel's cult. The significant role of blood in this cultic context is vividly evident in the technical term for the sin offering: "blood of sin" (דַּם חַטָּאת). The concept

---

9. Brown, *Gospel According to John*, 2. 937, 953. See also Heil, *Blood and Water*, 111–12. For a thorough discussion of the issue, see Menken, *Old Testament Quotations in the Fourth Gospel*, 147–66.

10. Though there is no doubt that John 19:37 is intended as a quotation of Zech 12:10, the relationship is not without complication. The version of the passage in the LXX does not employ piercing imagery and so could not have been the intended referent. But the MT version of Zech 12:10 as it appears in *BHS* reads "and they shall look upon *me* whom they have pierced" (וְהִבִּיטוּ אֵלַי אֵת אֲשֶׁר־דָּקָרוּ). Though there are a number of possible reasons for the difference between the MT version in *BHS* and the form of the passage quoted in John 19:37, two solutions are most commonly proposed. One of these solutions is that the author of the Gospel was quoting a version of Zech 12:10 that had a third person object. For a discussion regarding the extant MT manuscripts that have a third person object, see Jansma, *Zechariah IX–XIV*, 117–18. Another commonly proposed solution to the problem is that the author of the Gospel was thinking of a version of the OT passage with a first person object as in the MT of *BHS* but applying it to the present context changed the object to the third person (Menken, *Old Testament Quotations in the Fourth Gospel*, 179–80). Both of these proposals are plausible solutions and both have their advocates. Fortunately, while the issue is worthy of note given the relationship of Zech 12:10 to the present study, a resolution of the problem is not required for the study's interpretation of John 19:34. For more discussion, see Freed, *Old Testament Quotations in the Gospel of John*, 108–116; Menken, *Old Testament Quotations in the Fourth Gospel*, 167–85; and Tuckett, "Zech 12:10 and the New Testament," 111–21.

65

behind this ritual usage is well summarized in Leviticus: "For the life of the flesh is in its blood, and I have given it to you for purification for your lives upon the altar, for it is the blood, by its life, that purifies" (17:11). Much of the above imagery was adopted into the early Christian kerygma and is manifest in a number of passages in the NT where Jesus' blood is described as a life-giving substance that purifies from sin (see especially Heb 9:11–14, 23–28).

As discussed in chapter 3 of this study, the symbolism from the cultural milieu had an influence on the manner in which the word "blood" was employed in the Gospel. In the first occurrence, based upon the association with life, the symbol of blood was used as an image for natural birth (1:13). In the second occurrence, the blood of Jesus was described as a source of life which, given the cultural influence, appeared to imply a purificatory and life-giving function to his death (6:53–56). Thus, although the word "blood" is limited in use to only two passages in the Gospel preceding 19:34, it is evident that the symbolism of the surrounding culture had its influence.

WATER IN THE CULTURE AND GOSPEL PRECEDING 19:34

As demonstrated in chapter 2 of this study, there were also cultural presuppositions that would have influenced the intended audience when they heard about the flow of water in 19:34. In summary, water is portrayed in the Scriptures of Israel as a natural cleansing mechanism and an essential thirst-quenching sustenance of life. The cleansing quality of water was the basis for its use in various purification rituals, a cultic role characterized most clearly in the technical term "water of uncleanness" (מֵי נִדָּה).[11] The image of water as an essential sustenance of life figures significantly in the images of Israel's postexilic restoration. In that day "living water" was to flow from the eschatological temple—imagery that is itself symbolic of the eschatological outpouring of God's Spirit. Such OT symbolism was subsumed in the nascent Christian kerygma and is manifest most clearly in the NT passages that concern baptism (see especially 1 Cor 6:11; 12:12–13; Titus 3:5).

---

11. As discussed in chapter 4 of this study this cultic technical term was employed by the community behind the DSS as a description of their initiatory baptismal rite (1QS 3.3–5; 4.20–21; 5.13–14).

The Interpretation of John 19:34

As discussed in chapter 4 of this study, the symbolic significance of water in the culture of the intended audience influenced the use of the image of water in the Gospel preceding 19:34. Purification symbolism was employed in the stories about John's baptism (1:26, 31, 33; 3:23), the wedding at Cana (2:7, 9; 4:46), the dialogue with Nicodemus (3:5), and the washing of the disciples' feet (13:5). The image of water as a thirst-quenching sustenance of life was employed in the dialogue with the Samaritan woman (4:7, 10, 11, 13, 14, 15) and Jesus' words at the festival of Booths (7:38). In these latter two passages Jesus was portrayed as the eschatological temple flowing with "living water," and in the second passage this water was said to symbolize the Spirit that would be accessible after Jesus' glorification (7:39).

THE MEANING OF BLOOD AND WATER IN JOHN 19:34

The final occurrences of the words "blood" and "water" in the Gospel are in 19:34. It has already been demonstrated that the use of the words "blood" and "water" in the Gospel preceding 19:34 was influenced by their symbolic significance in the surrounding culture. It is reasonable to expect, therefore, that the author intended the words "blood and water" in 19:34 to be interpreted in like manner. Thus, the blood should be understood in relation to life and/or purification from sin and the water should be understood in relation to life and/or purification from uncleanness.

In fact, the earliest known commentary on the flow of blood and water from Jesus' side, attributed to Apollinaris of Hierapolis (2nd cent.), interprets the imagery as "two purifying streams" and seemingly, therefore, as the fulfillment of the purification requirements of the Mosaic Law.[12] Though such cultic interpretations of John 19:34 do not appear often in the subsequent history of exegesis, dominated as it is by sacramental interpretations, they are not absent entirely. For example, in the Reformation Era, as discussed in chapter 1 of this study, John Calvin concluded that the "blood and water" in John 19:34 were intended to demonstrate the fulfillment of the old law's cultic regulations regarding "sacrifices and washings."[13]

But such cultic interpretations are not limited to the precritical era. Brooke F. Westcott, whose interpretation was also discussed in chapter 1 of this study, understood the "blood and water" in John 19:34 to be cultic

---

12. The text is preserved in the preface of the seventh-century work *Chronicon Paschale* (*PG*, 92.79–80). For more discussion, see Bernard, *Gospel According to St. John*, 648.
13. Calvin, *In Evangelium Ioannes* (*Corpus Reformatorum*, 47.421).

symbols of a "double cleansing and vivifying power" demonstrating that the "Old Covenant" was fulfilled in the New.[14] Indeed, that the imagery in John 19:34 was intended to convey a fulfillment of cultic requirements, such that the blood refers to life and/or purification from sin and that the water refers to life and or/purification from uncleanness are interpretations found in many modern critical studies.[15] This is not surprising, since as Bruce H. Grigsby has summarized, "The cultic overtones of this incident are difficult to ignore."[16]

The problem, however, is that while there is indeed a growing consensus composed not only of a few ancient commentaries, but more importantly, numerous modern and well-supported critical analyses, all arguing that the imagery of John 19:34 was intended to convey the fulfillment of Mosaic cultic requirements or OT symbolism in general, there is very little consensus in precisely how this fulfillment was intended by the author in the particular details of John 19:34. The reason for this lack of consensus is that the author's intention regarding the nature of the relationship of the imagery of John 19:34 to the cult of Israel is not so easily perceived on the immediate surface of the text.

This difficulty is not insurmountable however, as the solution to the problem becomes apparent when one lends an attentive ear to the voice of the narrator in the Gospel. The event described in 19:34 is explicitly declared

---

14. Westcott, *Gospel According to St. John*, 279.

15. That the blood represents life, see Westcott, *Gospel According to St. John*, 279; Hoskyns, *Fourth Gospel*, 533; Brown, *Gospel According to John*, 2.954; Carson, *Gospel According to John*, 624; Stibbe, *John as Storyteller*, 118; Heil, *Blood and Water*, 106–7; Morris, *Gospel According to John*, 725; Jones, *Symbol of Water in the Gospel of John*, 211; Culpepper, *Gospel and Letters of John*, 237; and Lincoln, *Gospel According to Saint John*, 479. That the blood represents purification, see Westcott, *Gospel According to St. John*, 279; Hoskyns, *Fourth Gospel*, 533; Schnackenburg, *Das Johannesevagelium*, 3.345; Brown, *Gospel According to John*, 2.952; Carson, *Gospel According to John*, 624; and Heil, *Blood and Water*, 107. That the water represents life, see Westcott, *Gospel According to St. John*, 279; Schnackenburg, *Das Johannesevagelium*, 3.345; Brown, *Gospel According to John*, 2.954; Carson, *Gospel According to John*, 624; Stibbe, *John as Storyteller*, 118; Brodie, *Gospel According to John*, 552; Morris, *Gospel According to John*, 725; Lincoln, *Gospel According to Saint John*, 479; Koester, *Symbolism in the Fourth Gospel*, 203; and Jones, *Symbol of Water in the Gospel of John*, 211. That the water represents purification, see Westcott, *Gospel According to St. John*, 279; Hoskyns, *Fourth Gospel*, 533; Brown, *Gospel According to John*, 2.952; Carson, *Gospel According to John*, 624; Heil, *Blood and Water*, 106; and Koester, *Symbolism in the Fourth Gospel*, 201–2.

16. Grigsby, "Sacrifice in the Fourth Gospel," 61. Grigsby goes on to say, "Certainly, the description of outpoured blood indicates the Evangelist's awareness of an expiatory rationale between Christ's death and the removal of sin."

by the narrator in 19:37 to be the fulfillment of a "Scripture passage" that says, "They shall look at him whom they have pierced." As discussed already, it is evident that this is a reference to Zech 12:10. It is equally evident that the soldier's spear stab described in 19:34a is intended to be understood as the fulfillment of the piercing action in Zech 12:10. What is not so immediately evident, however, and what has led to the lack of consensus noted above, is the relationship of the resultant flow of "blood and water" in John 19:34b to this reference in Zechariah.[17] But the relationship of the "blood and water" becomes clear when the literary context of Zech 12:10 is examined carefully; as Raymond E. Brown has commented concerning this issue, "Here as elsewhere the NT author is citing a verse as evocative of a whole context."[18]

The immediate literary context of Zech 12:10, and for that matter the latter half of the book of Zechariah is a significant source of citations for the Gospel.[19] The words of Jesus during the cleansing of the temple (John 2:16) are an allusion to Zech 14:21.[20] Jesus' words to the Samaritan woman about "living water" (John 4:10–11) allude to the image of "living water" in Zech 14:8.[21] Jesus' declaration at the festival of Booths (John 7:37–39) is related to this same imagery of "living water" in Zech 14:8 and the depiction of the eschatological "festival of Booths" in Zech 14:16–17.[22] Jesus is described in shepherd imagery in John 10 that appears to be related to similar shepherd imagery in Zechariah 11.[23] The action of Jesus riding an ass into Jerusalem is said to fulfill Zech 9:9.[24] Jesus' words in John 16:32 are an allusion to the striking of the shepherd in Zech 13:7.[25] Finally, and most significantly for the present subject, the Gospel explicitly quotes from Zech 12:10 in

---

17. Bultmann saw this difficulty as an indication that 19:34b is a later addition (*Das Evangelium des Johannes*, 525 n. 4). His conclusion is unwarranted however, as is demonstrated below (see also the arguments contra Bultmann by Schnackenburg, *Das Johannesevangelium*, 3.335, and Brown, *Gospel According to John*, 2.945–50).

18. Brown, *Gospel According to John*, 2.955. See also the similar comment of de la Potterie, *The Hour of Jesus*, 143.

19. Brown, *Gospel According to John*, 2.954.

20. Menken, *Old Testament Quotations in the Fourth Gospel*, 197.

21. See chapter 4 of this study. See also Keener, *Gospel of John*, 1.604; and the detailed discussion in Allison, "Living Water," 143–57.

22. Brown, *Gospel According to John*, 2.954.

23. Ibid.

24. Ibid.

25. Ibid. See also Menken, *Old Testament Quotations in the Fourth Gospel*, 197.

Seeing Blood and Water

John 19:37 in reference to the imagery in John 19:34. As summarized by Maarten J. J. Menken who has made an extensive study of OT quotations in the Gospel: "John has an evident interest in Zechariah 9–14."[26]

Based, therefore, upon the symbolic significance of the images of blood and water in the cultural milieu, the influence of this symbolism in the uses of the words "blood" and "water" in the Gospel preceding 19:34, the influence of the latter part of Zechariah on the Gospel, and especially the explicit declaration of the narrator that the words of Zech 12:10 are fulfilled in the spear stab in John 19:34a, the present study concludes that the author of the Gospel expected the audience to understand the flow of "blood and water" in John 19:34 as the fulfillment of Zech 13:1, a verse that follows almost immediately after 12:10.[27] The relationship between Zech 12:10 and 13:1 in the original literary context of Zechariah is evident when the two verses are examined consecutively.[28]

> Zech 12:10 I will pour out on the house of David and on the inhabitants of Jerusalem a spirit of favor and supplication; and they shall look upon me/him[29] whom they have pierced, and they shall mourn for him as one mourns for an only son, and they shall grieve over him as one grieves over a firstborn.

> Zech 13:1 On that day a fountain shall be opened for the house of David and for the inhabitants of Jerusalem to purify from sin and uncleanness.

Zech 12:10 is certainly significant in its original literary context, but the importance of Zech 13:1 cannot be overemphasized. As it has been declared, "The claim of 13:1, through the use of these comprehensive technical terms ["sin and uncleanness"], is that total purification from any and all sins or

---

26. Menken, *Old Testament Quotations in the Fourth Gospel*, 197.

27. For commentators who have suggested a relationship between John 19:34 and the Hebrew text of Zech 13:1, see Henry, *Commentary*, 1015; Ryle, *Expository Thoughts on the Gospels*, 3.371–72; Brown, *Gospel According to John*, 2.954–55 (see also idem, *Death of the Messiah*, 2.1181); Barrett, *Gospel According to St. John*, 557; Minear, *John*, 78; de la Potterie, *Hour of Jesus*, 143–44; Carson, *Gospel According to John*, 628; Malina and Rohrbaugh, *Gospel of John*, 274–75; Ridderbos, *Gospel of John*, 623–24; and Lincoln, *Gospel According to Saint John*, 482.

28. Concerning the relationship between Zech 12:10 and 13:1, see Meyers and Meyers, *Zechariah 9–14*, 362, 398. See also Brown, *Gospel According to John*, 955; and de la Potterie, *Hour of Jesus*, 143–44.

29. Concerning the variation of the pronoun, see n. 10 above.

The Interpretation of John 19:34

defiling actions ... will be achieved."[30] The imagery of the verse, therefore, "provides a comprehensive conception of the state of pollution, caused by moral wrongdoing and contaminating activity that will be removed by the cosmic fountain in the future age."[31]

Based upon the importance of 13:1 in the book of Zechariah as well as the verse's literary relationship and proximity to Zech 12:10, it is reasonable to expect that the author of the Gospel, after having cited Zech 12:10 as the fulfillment of the spear stab in 19:34, would also intend the image of the flow from Jesus' side as the fulfillment of the purifying fountain in Zech 13:1.[32] But it becomes evident that this was in fact the author's intention when the effects of the purifying fountain and their order in Zech 13:1b are compared to the contents of the flow and their order in John 19:34b.

Zech 13:1b: ... sin (חַטָּאת) and uncleanness (נִדָּה).

John 19:34b: ... blood (αἷμα) and water (ὕδωρ).

---

30. Meyers and Meyers, *Zechariah 9–14*, 367.

31. Ibid., 366.

32. The study assumes that the author is thinking of the Hebrew text of Zech 13:1 and not the LXX version for the following reasons. First, the author's quotation of Zech 12:10 in John 19:37 is based on the Hebrew text and not on the LXX (see n. 10 above). If the author were to use another passage in Zechariah dependent upon the use of Zech 12:10, e.g., Zech 13:1 as is suggested by this and a number of other studies (see n. 27 above), it is reasonable to expect that the Hebrew text would be employed again in the case of the dependent passage. Second, like the LXX version of Zech 12:10, the LXX version of 13:1 does not include imagery advantageous to the present Gospel context, as it contains only a translation of 13:1a (see Ziegler, *Duodecim prophetae*, 321). The Hebrew version of 13:1, however, does include imagery advantageous to the present Gospel context and it would be surprising therefore, if the author would not make use of this imagery, especially since the audience's knowledge of the Hebrew text has already been assumed by the author. The author's intentional transition from the use of the LXX to a Hebrew version of a particular passage for the purpose of preferred imagery advantageous to the Gospel context is a technique manifest in the immediate context (i.e., Zech 12:10) and is evidenced elsewhere in the Gospel. As Maarten J. J. Menken has stated, "The evangelist's use of the LXX does not exclude an occasional recourse to the Hebrew text. ... It is important to observe that ... where John evidently did not quote from the LXX, good reasons can be adduced for his not doing so" (*Old Testament Quotations in the Fourth Gospel*, 205). For more discussion regarding the author's recourse to the Hebrew text, see Barrett, *Gospel According to St. John*, 28; Freed, *Old Testament Quotations in the Gospel of John*, 126; and Menken, *Old Testament Quotations in the Fourth Gospel*, 205–7. See also Moloney's comment cited above (chapter 1, n. 81) regarding the bicultural appeal of the Gospel. For other arguments concerning specifically the relationship of John 19:34 to Zech 13:1, see the comments of those cited in n. 27 above.

Seeing Blood and Water

With this correlation, the "blood" (αἷμα) provides the prophesied purification of "sin" (חַטָּאת), and the "water" (ὕδωρ) provides the prophesied purification of "uncleanness" (נִדָּה).[33]

Such a correlation was probably assumed by the author to have been obvious enough for the audience based upon the symbolic significance of blood and water from the cultural milieu. But it was probably assumed obvious for another reason as well, and that is the literary relationship of the word "blood" (αἷμα [דָּם]) with the word "sin" (חַטָּאת) and the word "water" (ὕδωρ [מַיִם]) with the word "uncleanness" (נִדָּה) in the cultic technical terms in the Mosaic Law, "blood of sin" (דַּם חַטָּאת) and "water of uncleanness" (מֵי נִדָּה).

In summary, the author of the Gospel could have expected with relative certainty that the intended audience would perceive a relationship between the "blood and water" from Jesus' side and the cultic concepts of purification of "sin and uncleanness" based upon the symbolic significance of blood and water in the cultural milieu. Indeed, that the author expected such an association is suggested by the employment of this symbolic significance on the use of the words "blood" and "water" in the Gospel preceding 19:34. When, therefore, the narrator described "blood and water" coming forth from Jesus' side in 19:34 and then explicitly cited Zech 12:10, it could be assumed that the audience would understand that the flow of "blood and water" from Jesus' side fulfilled the image of the fountain purifying of "sin and uncleanness" in Zech 13:1. To be sure, such a conclusion was virtually inescapable in light of the already existent literary relationship of the words "blood" and "sin" and the words "water" and "uncleanness" in the cultic technical terms in the Mosaic Law, "blood of sin" and "water of uncleanness."

The author of Zechariah 13:1 employed the imagery of a purifying fountain to show that in the eschatological day God would purify all "sin and uncleanness" and thereby bring about perfect fulfillment of the requirements of the Mosaic Law. Likewise, the author of the Gospel, who had already borrowed heavily from Zechariah in the Gospel preceding 19:34, intended to demonstrate in 19:34, by the description of the stabbing of Jesus' side and the "blood and water" that flowed out, that Jesus' death

---

33. Incidentally, though the present study has arrived at this conclusion independently, this interpretation of John 19:34 and its relationship to Zech 13:1 is also found in the commentaries of Ryle, *Expository Thoughts on the Gospels*, 3.371–72; and Minear, *John*, 78.

fulfilled not only the imagery of Zech 12:10 but the image in Zech 13:1 as well, and thus provides the prophesied purification of all "sin and uncleanness" for those who believe in him.

But if the flow of blood and water from Jesus' side shows that he provides the fulfillment of Zech 13:1, then another conclusion regarding the imagery of 19:34 is possible as well. Zech 13:1 plays a significant role in the latter half of Zechariah and, as such, is related not only to 12:10 but also 14:8.[34] The relationship between 13:1 and 14:8a is particularly evident in the parallel language:

> Zech 13:1 On that day a fountain shall be opened for the house of David and for the inhabitants of Jerusalem to purify from sin and uncleanness.

> Zech 14:8 On that day living water shall flow from Jerusalem, half to the eastern sea, and half to the western sea, and it shall be so in summer and in winter.

The words "On that day" at the beginning of both verses helps to emphasize the relationship, so that the "fountain" (מָקוֹר) in 13:1 anticipates the description of the flow of "living water" (מַיִם־חַיִּים) in 14:8.[35] What becomes clear when the two verses are compared is that both describe the same concept of "cosmic waters" flowing from the eschatological temple.[36] Due to this anticipatory relationship between Zech 13:1 and 14:8, it is reasonable to expect that the author of the Gospel who had already made use of the relationship between Zech 12:10 and 13:1 would also make use of the relationship between Zech 13:1 and 14:8. In fact, there are two significant indications that this was the case.

First, it has already been shown that the images of blood and water have a twofold symbolic significance of life and purification in the surrounding

---

34. Meyers and Meyers, *Zechariah 9-14*, 362-63.

35. For the structural role of the words "on that day" in this latter part of Zechariah and the relationship of the word מָקוֹר in 13:1 and the words מַיִם־חַיִּים in 14:8 see Meyers and Meyers, *Zechariah 9-14*, 362.

36. Meyers and Meyers, *Zechariah 9-14*, 362, 434. Interestingly enough, a relationship exists between the technical term "water of uncleanness" and the image of "living water" not only here in Zechariah but in the Mosaic Law as well (compare Num 19:17 with 19:9, 13, 20, 21; and 31:23). See also the similar dual imagery in the image of life-giving water in Ezek 47:9 and the purificatory water in 36:25, 29. For more discussion of the relevance of the eschatological temple motif in postexilic prophetic literature, see Meyers and Meyers, "Jerusalem and Zion After the Exile," 121-35.

culture. It has also already been shown that this twofold significance influenced the author of the Gospel in the use of the words "blood" and "water" preceding 19:34. The purification aspect of this complex of symbolism is employed in John 19:34 as the fulfillment of Zech 13:1. It is likely, therefore, that the aspect of life in this complex of symbolism would be employed as well, and this is in fact the very aspect that appears in the image of "living water" in Zech 14:8.

Second, the author has already made use of Zech 14:8 in both the dialogue with the Samaritan woman and Jesus' words at the festival of Booths when Jesus was described as the eschatological temple that would flow with "living water" (4:10, 11; 7:38). It is likely that this image might be employed again since the narrator had already declared in the latter passage that the imagery of "living water" was related to the coming glorification of Jesus (7:39).

Based, therefore, upon the anticipatory relationship between Zech 13:1 and 14:8, the symbolic significance of blood and water in relation to both purification and life, and the author's use of the "living water" imagery of Zech 14:8 earlier in the Gospel, this study also concludes that John 19:34 was intended not only as the fulfillment of Zech 12:10 and 13:1 but also, like in the relationship between Zech 13:1 and 14:8, as a narrative anticipation of the post-resurrection event described in John 20:19–23.

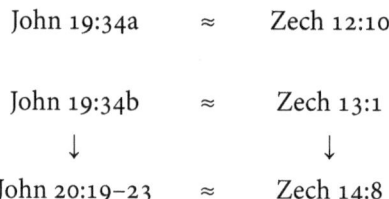

In fulfillment of Zech 13:1, the flow from Jesus' side was shown to be a purifying fountain fulfilling the cultic requirements of the Mosaic Law, but in anticipation of John 20:19–23, it also shows the relationship between this purifying fountain and the flow of the Holy Spirit—the "living water" of Zech 14:8.[37]

---

37. That the symbolic value of the images of blood and water are to be interpreted in combination and thus as a single flow and unified symbolic image, see Schnackenburg, *Das Johannesevagelium*, 3. 345; de la Potterie, *Hour of Jesus*, 142; Stibbe, *John as Storyteller*, 118; Heil, *Blood and Water*, 106; and Jones, *Symbol of Water in the Gospel of John*, 211.

The Interpretation of John 19:34

The author of the Gospel was careful to show that in the narrative future of the dialogue with the Samaritan woman, Jesus as the eschatological temple would give "living water." This was confirmed again in the narrator's declaration in the story about the festival of Booths, but as it was said there, Jesus' words regarding the "living water" would not be fulfilled until Jesus had been glorified (7:39). The glorification of Jesus has now begun and so the "living water" he promised is shown now to be accessible.[38]

But how is this "living water" accessible? Or for that matter, how is the eschatological purification of sin and uncleanness accessible? How is it that the believer benefits from the death of Jesus that gives both purification and life? The answer was given earlier in the same narrative describing the declaration at the festival of Booths. There it was explained by the narrator that "living water" was a metaphor for the "Spirit" (7:39).

Through the Spirit the believer has access to both the purification and life made possible by the death of Jesus.[39] For in this Gospel it is the Spirit that purifies from sin and uncleanness (1:33; 3:5; 20:22–23) and it is the living water, or Spirit, that gives life.[40] The coming gift of the Spirit is signaled by the dramatic flow from Jesus side in 19:34 and thus as the fulfillment of the eschatological visions of Zechariah. But, as in the relationship between Zech 13:1 and 14:8, it also anticipates the post-resurrection event, when Jesus breathed the Spirit upon his disciples (John 20:21–24). As declared by Heil,

> That they receive the holy Spirit made available by Jesus' death proceeds from his showing them his side (πλευράν) (20:20)—the same pierced side (πλευράν) out of which flowed the blood and

---

38. For commentators who have suggested a relationship between John 7:37–39 and 19:34, and for more discussion of the issue, see Dodd, *Interpretation of the Fourth Gospel*, 438; Schnackenburg, *Das Johannesevagelium*, 3. 345; Brodie, *Gospel According to John*, 552; Moloney, *Gospel of John*, 505; Culpepper, *Gospel and Letters of John*, 237; Brown, *Death of the Messiah*, 2. 1181; Heil, *Blood and Water*, 106–7; and Koester, *Symbolism in the Fourth Gospel*, 201.

39. For those who have suggested that there is a relationship between 19:34 and the gift of the Spirit, see Malatesta, "Blood and Water," 175; Vellanickal, "Blood and Water," 222–23, 228; de la Potterie, "Le Symbolisme du sang et de l'eau en Jn 19,34," 211–13 (see also idem, *Hour of Jesus*, 142–43); Heil, *Blood and Water*, 106–7; Keener, *Gospel of John*, 2. 1153; Koester, *Symbolism in the Fourth Gospel*, 203; and Jones, *Symbol of Water in the Gospel of John*, 211, 17.

40. For more discussion concerning the relationship of the Spirit and purification in the Gospel, see Keener, *Divine Purity*, 135–62.

Seeing Blood and Water

water (19:34), the 'rivers of living water' that symbolize the Life-giving Spirit (7:38–39).[41]

Through Jesus, the eschatological temple flowing with living water and purification, the Spirit that the disciples receive enables those who believe "to worship the Father in Spirit and truth, transcending the worship of Mount Gerizim and in the temple of Jerusalem (4:20–24)."[42]

SACRAMENTAL SYMBOLISM

As already discussed in chapter 3 of this study, the relationship of the Fourth Gospel to early Christian sacramentology has been the subject of much debate over the last century.[43] As was also already discussed, one of the early and most influential voices for a minimalist position in this regard was that of Rudolf Bultmann. His position held that the Gospel is in fact antisacramental, and if there is any reference to early Christian sacramental praxis it is found only in later ecclesiastical additions in 3:5 (baptism), 6:51–58 (Eucharist), and 19:34 (baptism and Eucharist).[44]

The sacramental question concerning 3:5 was addressed in chapter 4 of this study. It was demonstrated, given the preceding narrative and the cultural backdrop of the Gospel, that the description of a new birth by water and the Spirit was most likely intended as an allusion to a rite of baptism.[45] As Larry P. Jones has commented in his study of water symbolism in the Gospel, "A reader familiar with Christian tradition would have difficulty not finding references to the practice of baptism throughout the passage."[46] The narrative concerning Nicodemus is significant for the present issue,

---

41. Heil, *Blood and Water*, 138. Brown made a similar point when he said, "The symbolism here is proleptic and serves to clarify that, while only the risen Jesus gives the Spirit, that gift flows from the whole process of glorification in 'the hour' of the passion, death, resurrection, and ascension" (*Gospel According to John*, 2. 951). See also Burge, *Holy Spirit in the Johannine Tradition*, 133–35.

42. Heil, *Blood and Water*, 138.

43. For a summary of the debate, see Brown, "The Johannine Sacramentary Reconsidered," 183–206; idem, *New Testament Essays*, 51–95; Moloney, "When Is John Talking about Sacraments," 10–33; and Barrett, *Essays on John*, 37–97.

44. Bultmann, *Das Evangelium des Johannes*, 98 n. 2, 174, 525.

45. For a short summary of the issue, see Burge, *The Holy Spirit in the Johannine Tradition*, 166–67.

46. Jones, *Symbolism of Water in John*, 75. See also the similar comment of Schnackenburg, *Das Johannesevangelium*, 1.383.

however, not only because of this allusion to water baptism but also because it contains a dramatic reference to the coming crucifixion: "And just as Moses lifted up the serpent in the wilderness, so must the Son of man be lifted up, that whoever believes in him may have eternal life" (3:14–15).[47]

John 6:51–58, the second of the three sacramental passages allowed by Bultmann's minimalist position, was addressed in chapter 3 of this study. It was demonstrated there, as it had already been argued by many before,[48] that the words describing the eating of Jesus' flesh and the drinking of his blood were related in some degree to the eucharistic practice of the intended audience. The discourse on the Bread of Life is significant for the present issue, however, not only because of this allusion to the Eucharist, but also because like the Nicodemus narrative it contains a dramatic reference to the coming crucifixion: "Then what if you were to see the Son of Man going up to where he was before?" (6:62).[49]

The last of the three sacramental passages allowed by Bultmann's minimalist position is 19:34. Since 19:34 is the climactic scene in the Johannine passion narrative, and the other two passages allowed by Bultmann's minimalist position both point to the crucifixion, it is reasonable to expect that there might be some relationship between the sacramental imagery in these two passages and that of 19:34. This expectation is even more reasonable given the commonality of terms ("water" [3:5], "blood" [6:53, 54, 55, 56], "blood and water" [19:34]).

The commentaries of Calvin and Westcott were cited above as examples of interpretations of the "blood and water" in John 19:34 as signs that the death of Jesus brought about the fulfillment of the purification requirements of the Mosaic Law. But their interpretations are also relevant for the present issue since both of these interpreters concluded that the words "blood and water" in 19:34 were also related to the sacraments of Eucharist and baptism, respectively. As it was demonstrated in chapter 1 of

---

47. For more discussion, see Matera, *New Testament Christology*, 233–34.

48. See, for example, Bernard, *Gospel According to St. John*, 1.212; Hoskyns, *Fourth Gospel*, 304; Lightfoot, *St. John's Gospel*, 162; Bultmann, *Das Evangelium des Johannes*, 174; Barrett, *Gospel According to St. John*, 297; Dodd, *Interpretation of the Fourth Gospel*, 338; Schnackenburg, *Das Johannesevangelium*, 2.85. Brown, *Gospel According to John*, 1.284–85; Brodie, *Gospel According to John*, 286; Moloney, *Gospel of John*, 223–24; Culpepper, *Gospel and Letters of John*, 163; Keener, *Gospel of John*, 1.689–91; Lincoln, *Gospel According to Saint John*, 232–35; Neyrey, *Gospel of John*, 127. For studies of NT eucharistic imagery that have concluded likewise, see especially Jeremias, *Eucharistic Words*, 107; Kilpatrick, *Eucharist*, 55; and Kodell, *Eucharist*, 121–26.

49. See discussion in Matera, *New Testament Christology*, 234.

this study, the overwhelmingly dominant interpretation of this verse in the history of exegesis is that there is some relationship between John 19:34 and the sacraments of the intended audience, and this line of interpretation has been maintained and refined by a number of modern scholars.[50]

One of the more recent influential advocates of a sacramental interpretation has been Francis J. Moloney, who has said regarding the subject,

> If pre-Johannine Christianity shows that *at least* Eucharist and Baptism were central in early Christian worship, then it seems logical that the author of the Fourth Gospel would show that these Sacraments had their basis in the words and works of Jesus.[51]

Accordingly, Moloney has interpreted the imagery of John 19:34 as follows: "The life-giving Sacraments of Eucharist and Baptism, are described as flowing down upon the nascent Church from the King, lifted up upon his throne."[52]

But a sacramental interpretation such as this raises a question. If an allusion to the sacraments was intended, where the water is representative of baptism and the blood is representative of Eucharist, shouldn't the text say that "water and blood" flowed out, not "blood and water"? Initiatory baptism would have certainly preceded participation in the eucharistic meal in the experience of the intended audience, and it is reasonable to expect that this order would be reflected in John 19:34, if it was indeed intended as an allusion to these sacraments.[53]

It has already been demonstrated that the words "blood and water" in 19:34 were ordered to correspond to the words "sin and uncleanness" in Zech 13:1. But this correspondence to Zechariah does not necessarily

---

50. For modern commentators who have suggested the possibility of a sacramental interpretation, see Westcott, *Gospel According to St. John*, 279; Hoskyns, *Fourth Gospel*, 533; Lightfoot, *St. John's Gospel*, 320; Bultmann, *Das Evangelium des Johannes*, 525; Brown, "Johannine Sacramentary Reconsidered," 206 (see also idem, *Gospel According to John*, 2.952); Barrett, *Gospel According to St. John*, 557; Malatesta, "Blood and Water," 175; Vellanickal, "Blood and Water," 228; Brodie, *Gospel According to John*, 553; Heil, *Blood and Water*, 108-9; and Moloney, "When is John Talking about the Sacraments," 25 (see also idem, *Gospel of John*, 505-6).

51. Moloney, "When is John Talking About Sacraments," 14.

52. Ibid., 25.

53. Schnackenburg, *Das Johannesevagelium*, 3.345. Another question is also sometimes raised regarding the possibility that the word "blood" by itself could be a reference to the Eucharist (ibid). But this problem does not present as significant an obstacle as the problem of order, since it may be argued that this is simply a unique occurrence of a uniquely Johannine usage.

The Interpretation of John 19:34

exclude the possibility that a sacramental interpretation of John 19:34 was intended. On the contrary, the appropriation of this eschatological imagery of Zechariah may be the strongest indication that a sacramental interpretation was indeed expected.

As it has been shown, the imagery in John 19:34 is intended to demonstrate that the death of Jesus fulfills the eschatological purification of "sin and uncleanness" foreseen in Zech 13:1 and the eschatological life provided by the "living water" foreseen in Zech 14:8. But how is this purification and life accessible? The answer is the Spirit, as was demonstrated above. In this Gospel it is the Spirit that purifies from sin and uncleanness (1:33; 3:5; 20:22–23) and it is the Spirit that gives life (6:63).[54] For the Gospel's intended audience any potential power of the sacraments would have been intimately associated with the power of the Spirit. As Frank J. Matera has commented concerning the Johannine image of baptism:

> Those who enter the community are "born from above" through the power of the Spirit, which is given to them through water baptism in Jesus' name. Baptism, then, is the sacrament of *water and the Spirit*, water signifying the "living water" that is the Spirit. It is not simply a rite of washing but a sign that points to the living water that is the Spirit.[55]

The same can be said concerning the eucharistic meal. As Matera has also described the Johannine image of Eucharist:

> The Eucharist is the way in which believers appropriate Jesus, the bread of life that has come down from heaven. When they believe in him as the bread that has come down from heaven and eat his flesh and drink his blood in the Eucharist, they have life in themselves and the promise of future resurrection life.[56]

The sacramental presence of Jesus as the bread of life that has come down from heaven in the eucharistic meal is a presence made possible by the power of the Spirit. The ability of the participant to believe in Jesus as the bread that has come down from heaven is a gift made possible by the same power of the Spirit. Likewise, the life the believer receives and the promise of future resurrection life are things made possible by the power of the

---

54. For the relationship of the Spirit to purification in the Gospel, see Keener, *Divine Purity*, 135–62.

55. Matera, *New Testament Theology*, 308–9.

56. Ibid., 310.

Spirit as well. In summary, through this life-giving power of the Spirit in the eucharistic meal, the "sacramental food and drink resulting from the death of Jesus nourishes and unites the community of believers ... with the eternal life Jesus shares with the Father."[57]

Thus, while it may be difficult, due to the difference in order, to establish the existence of a direct relationship between the words "blood and water" in 19:34 and the sacraments of Eucharist and baptism respectively, it is also equally difficult to deny, as even the minimalist position of Bultmann determined, that some sacramental relationship exists.

The primary purpose of the imagery in 19:34 is to show that Jesus' death fulfilled the piercing, purificatory, and life-giving elements prophesied in the eschatological imagery of Zech 12:10 and its immediate literary context. But because of the relationship of this imagery to the eschatological outpouring of the power of the Spirit and the relationship of the power of the Spirit to the sacraments of the intended audience a relationship appears to exist through the role of the Spirit—the Spirit is that which purifies and it is the Spirit that gives life.[58]

CONCLUSION

The first two chapters of the present study summarized the history of interpretation of John 19:34, examined the manuscript tradition of this verse along with its immediate literary context (19:31–37), and supplied a summary of the symbolic significance of the images of blood and water in the cultural milieu of the Gospel. The next two chapters of the study showed how this symbolic significance influenced the manner in which the words "blood" and "water" were employed in the Gospel preceding 19:34. The present chapter has completed the study's analysis of this imagery with a focused examination of John 19:34 in its immediate literary context (19:31–37). The study has shown that the symbolic significance from the surrounding culture that had already influenced the use of the words "blood" and "water" in the Gospel preceding 19:34, comparably influenced the use of these words in 19:34.

---

57. Heil, *Blood and Water*, 108. See also the similar comment of Schnackenburg, *Das Johannesevangelium*, 2. 94–95.

58. For similar arguments and more discussion, see Brown, *Gospel According to John*, 2. 952; Barrett, *Gospel According to St. John*, 557; and Brodie, *Gospel According to John*, 553.

Thus, it has been demonstrated that the author intended the imagery of John 19:34 to be related not only to Zech 12:10, as is explicitly declared in John 19:37, but also to the immediate literary context of Zech 12:10, specifically 13:1, where the "blood and water" was shown to fulfill the purificatory requirements of the Mosaic Law regarding "sin and uncleanness." But just as Zech 13:1 anticipated the flow of "living water" from the eschatological temple in Zech 14:8, the flow of "blood and water" (John 19:34b) was shown to anticipate the flow of the Holy Spirit from Jesus (John 20:19–23). As it had already been described earlier in the Gospel, Jesus was indeed the fulfillment of the eschatological temple that would flow with "living water" when glorified (John 7:37–39) and, as was demonstrated, this language was intended to symbolize the outpouring of the Spirit.

The chapter also illustrated how the study's findings assist in answering questions about the relationship of John 19:34 to the sacramental life of the Gospel's intended audience. The chapter explained that while a primary sacramental interpretation may be difficult to establish due to the lack of correspondence to sacramental order, the existence of some relationship to the sacraments is surely plausible when the role of the Spirit is taken into account.

The next and final chapter summarizes the investigations and findings of this study and discusses the study's potential impact on subsequent Johannine research and modern critical study of the NT. The chapter concludes with a few suggestions for future research regarding two other NT passages related to John 19:34 and the Jewish literary traditions regarding the wilderness rock, and illustrates how the conclusions of the present study may assist in this research.

6

Closing Remarks

INTRODUCTION

THE PREVIOUS CHAPTERS OF this study provided a comprehensive narrative-critical analysis of John 19:34. This final chapter summarizes the study's method, findings, and conclusions, and demonstrates how the study contributes to modern critical research of the Fourth Gospel. The chapter then closes with recommendations for future research regarding imagery similar to that of John 19:34 in two other NT passages and in Jewish literary traditions regarding the wilderness rock.

SUMMARY OF THE STUDY

Chapter 1 of this study provided a general introduction to the history of interpretation of John 19:34. As demonstrated, the various interpretations of this verse in exegetical literature from the early patristic period to the present comprise a massive literary body.

In the ante-Nicene period John 19:34 was frequently interpreted as the fulfillment of OT imagery such as the wilderness rock that gave water (Exod 17:1–7; Num 20:2–13) and the salvific red cloth hanging from Rahab's window (Josh 2:18). The ante-Nicene interpreters also suggested associations with various elements of the Christian kerygma such as the power of the Holy Spirit, the birth of the Church, and the sacraments of

Closing Remarks

Eucharist and baptism. From the post-Nicene period through the Reformation the vast majority of interpretations of John 19:34 did little more than restate previous interpretations.

In the post-Reformation era, however, a new stage in biblical interpretation arose as scholars began to explore outside the bounds of Christian literature for exegetical assistance. With this new direction in biblical studies innovative ideas began to emerge regarding John 19:34 and in time a large body of fresh exegetical material had been amassed.

As demonstrated in chapter 1, this body of material has grown dramatically in recent decades. The problem, however, was that until the present study no comprehensive literary analysis had been devoted solely to John 19:34. As chapter 1 explained, the present study was undertaken for the purpose of resolving this problem by providing a thorough narrative-critical analysis of this key verse.

Chapter 2 of this study discussed the manuscript tradition of the text of John 19:31–37, the pericope in which this verse appears, offered an English translation, and provided an analysis of the pericope's literary structure. Anticipating that there might be some relationship to the imagery in John 19:34, the chapter also included an examination of the symbolic significance of the images of blood and water in the cultural milieu of the Gospel's intended audience.

The examination revealed that there were indeed cultural presuppositions that would have influenced the intended audience when they heard about the flow of blood in John 19:34. The Scriptures of Israel describe blood as the seat of life. Based upon this concept, blood was used for the ritual purification of sin, a cultic role clearly manifest in the technical term for the sin offering: "blood of sin" (דַּם חַטָּאת).

The concept behind this ritual usage is well summarized in Leviticus: "For the life of the flesh is in its blood, and I have given it to you for purification for your lives upon the altar, for it is the blood, by its life, that purifies" (17:11). The symbolic significance of blood in the OT was adopted into the early Christian kerygma and is manifest in a number of passages in the NT where Jesus' blood is described as a life-giving substance that purifies from sin (see especially Heb 9:11–14, 23–28).

Having completed the investigation of the symbolic significance of the image of blood in the surrounding culture, the study then examined the significance of the image of water. The investigation revealed that there were, indeed, also cultural presuppositions that would have influenced the intended audience when they heard about the flow of water in 19:34. Water is portrayed in the Scriptures of Israel as a natural cleansing mechanism and an essential thirst-quenching sustenance of life. The cleansing quality of water was the basis for its use in various purification rituals, a cultic role clearly manifest in the technical term "water of uncleanness" (מֵי נִדָּה).

The image of water as an essential sustenance of life figures significantly in the images of Israel's postexilic restoration. In that day "living water" was to flow from the eschatological temple—imagery that is itself symbolic of the eschatological outpouring of God's Spirit. The OT symbolic significance of water as well as its association with God's Spirit was adopted into the nascent Christian kerygma and is manifested most clearly in the NT passages that concern baptism (see especially 1 Cor 6:11; 12:12–13; Titus 3:5).

Since it is reasonable to expect that the symbolic significance of blood and water from the surrounding culture would have had an influence on the use of the words "blood" and "water" in the Gospel, the next two chapters of the study were devoted to an investigation of the occurrences of the words "blood" and "water" preceding 19:34.

Chapter 3 of this study demonstrated that the symbolism from the cultural milieu had an influence on the manner in which the word "blood" was employed in the Gospel. In the first occurrence, based upon its association with life, the word "blood" was used in a metaphor for natural birth (1:13). In the second occurrence the "blood" of Jesus was described as a source of life which, given the cultural influence, appeared to imply a purificatory and life-giving function to his death (6:53–56). Thus, although the word "blood" is found only in two passages in the Gospel preceding 19:34, it is evident that the symbolic significance of the image of blood from the surrounding culture had its influence.

Chapter 4 of this study investigated the occurrences of the word "water" in the Gospel preceding 19:34. It was revealed that purification symbolism was employed in the stories about John's baptism (1:26, 31, 33; 3:23), the wedding at Cana (2:7, 9; 4:46), the dialogue with Nicodemus (3:5), and the washing of the disciples' feet (13:5). The image of water as a thirst-quenching sustenance of life was employed in the dialogue with the Samaritan woman (4:7, 10, 11, 13, 14, 15) and Jesus' words at the festival of Booths (7:38). In these latter two passages Jesus was portrayed as the eschatological temple flowing with "living water," and in the second passage this water was said to symbolize the Spirit that would be accessible after

Jesus' glorification (7:39). Thus, it was evident, as in the case of the image of blood in the cultural milieu, that the symbolic significance of the image of water influenced the use of the word "water" in the Gospel preceding 19:34.

Based upon the conclusions of Chapters 3 and 4, it was logical to expect that the symbolic significance of the images of blood and water from the surrounding culture that had already influenced the use of the words "blood" and "water" in the Gospel preceding 19:34 comparably influenced the use of the words "blood and water" in 19:34.

The study then proceeded, in chapter 5, to a focused examination of 19:34 in its immediate literary context (19:31–37). In 19:37 the narrator declares that the prophetic utterance, "They shall look at him whom they have pierced" (Zech 12:10), was fulfilled by the event in John 19:34. The study demonstrated that this quotation of Zech 12:10 was intended to evoke related imagery in its immediate literary context, specifically that of Zech 13:1 and 14:8.

In 13:1 the visionary of Zechariah describes the image of a fountain flowing from the eschatological temple and purifying from "sin and uncleanness." The image is a prophetic symbol that expressed Israel's post-exilic hope for a future purification that would fulfill the requirements of the Mosaic Law concerning "sin and uncleanness" in the eschatological age. Chapter 2 of this study revealed that there were conceptual associations of blood with the purification of sin and water with the purification of uncleanness in the cultural milieu of the Gospel. It also revealed that there were literary links between the words "blood" and "sin" and "water" and "uncleanness" in the technical terms "blood of sin" (חַטָּאת דַּם) and "water of uncleanness" (מֵי נִדָּה) in the Mosaic Law. Chapters 3 and 4 of this study demonstrated that these conceptual and literary associations influenced the occurrences of the words "blood" and "water" in the Gospel preceding 19:34.

The study concluded in chapter 5, therefore, that the image of a flow of "blood and water" in 19:34 was intended to demonstrate that, through his glorification (i.e., his death, resurrection, and ascent to the Father), Jesus fulfilled not only Zech 12:10 but also the image of a fountain purifying of "sin and uncleanness" in 13:1 as well. As such, Jesus as the eschatological temple provides the fulfillment of the purification requirements of the Mosaic Law concerning "sin and uncleanness" foreseen in Zech 13:1.

In 14:8 the prophetic visionary of Zechariah also said that "living water" would flow from the eschatological temple, an image that expressed

Seeing Blood and Water

Israel's post-exilic hope for restoration and abundance of new life in the age to come. Based upon the associations of blood and water with life in the cultural milieu and the descriptions of Jesus as a source of "living water" earlier in the Gospel (4:10; 7:37–39), it was concluded that the image of the flow of "blood and water" in 19:34 was also intended to show that, through his glorification, Jesus fulfilled not only Zech 12:10 and 13:1 but also 14:8. As such, Jesus as the eschatological temple provides abundant life in the eschatological age and thus would also fulfill the prophetic image in Zech 14:8.

But how does the believer access the eschatological life and purification from sin and uncleanness provided by Jesus? The answer was given in the narrator's comment concerning the dramatic declaration at the feast of Booths. There it was explained that the "living water" was a metaphor for the "Spirit" that would be accessible once Jesus was glorified (7:39). Through the Spirit the believer has access to the eschatological gifts provided by Jesus' glorification since it is the Spirit that purifies from sin and uncleanness (1:33; 3:5; 20:22–23) and it is the Spirit that gives life (6:63).

The eschatological outpouring of the Spirit is anticipated by the flow from Jesus' side in 19:34 and thus as the fulfillment of the eschatological visions of Zechariah (i.e., 13:1 and 14:8), and then dramatically described after the resurrection when Jesus breathed the Spirit upon his disciples (John 20:21–24).

The disciples' reception of the Spirit is shown to be dependent upon Jesus' death and the process of glorification, as this post-resurrection giving of the Spirit is immediately preceded by Jesus revealing his pierced side (20:20)—the same side out of which flowed blood and water (19:34).[1] The Spirit that the disciples receive through Jesus, the eschatological temple flowing with life and purification from sin and uncleanness, enables those who believe in him to worship the Father "in Spirit and truth" (4:24)—an eschatological worship that transcends the worship on Mount Gerizim and that of the temple in Jerusalem (4:20–24).[2]

Based upon this conclusion regarding the relationship of the imagery of 19:34 to the eschatological outpouring of the Spirit, chapter 5 then demonstrated how the study's findings assist in answering questions regarding the relationship of 19:34 to the sacramental life of the Gospel's intended audience. While it may be difficult to establish the existence of a direct

---

1. Heil, *Blood and Water*, 138.
2. Ibid.

Closing Remarks

relationship between the words "blood and water" in 19:34 and the sacraments of Eucharist and baptism, respectively, it is equally difficult to deny, as even the minimalist position of Bultmann determined, that some sacramental relationship exists.[3]

As the study demonstrated, the imagery in 19:34 was intended to show that Jesus' death fulfilled the piercing, purificatory, and life-giving elements prophesied in the eschatological imagery of Zech 12:10 and its immediate literary context, i.e., 13:1 and 14:8. Since this eschatological imagery would have been understood as symbolic of the eschatological power of the Spirit by the Gospel's intended audience, and the intended audience would have understood the sacraments of baptism and Eucharist as purificatory and life-giving elements empowered by the Spirit, a definite relationship does indeed appear to exist and is manifest at the very least in the commonality of the role of the power of the Spirit.

CONTRIBUTIONS TO CRITICAL RESEARCH

The conclusions of the present study, just summarized, result in significant contributions to the modern critical study of the Fourth Gospel. Previous studies have been conducted concerning Johannine symbolism, and a few were devoted specifically to water symbolism in the Gospel. Building upon this earlier research, this study contributes to the interpretation of Johannine symbolism by providing another treatment of water symbolism in the Gospel that further confirms a number of the conclusions of earlier studies.

But in addition to confirming existing conclusions, this study has also contributed something new to the study of Johannine symbolism. Prior to the present study, very little research had been devoted to blood symbolism in the Gospel. This study has contributed to the research of Johannine symbolism by providing the most extensive investigation of blood symbolism in the Gospel to date. As such it has laid a firm foundation for future treatments of this subject.

More significantly, though many earlier studies suggested that there is a relationship between John 19:34 and the literary context of Zech 12:10, i.e., 13:1 and 14:8, the present study has provided substantial scientific support for this hypothesis. This has been accomplished in four ways.

First, by a thorough analysis of the symbolic significance of the images of blood and water in the cultural milieu the study demonstrated the

---

3. Bultmann, *Das Evangelium des Johannes*, 525.

existence of a strong conceptual relationship between the image of blood and the concepts of life and purification from sin and the image of water and the concepts of life and purification from uncleanness.

Second, by analyzing the use of the words "blood" and "water" in the Gospel, the study demonstrated that, through the author's employment of the cultural associations with blood and water, these associations were assumed to be apparent to the intended audience when they occurred again in 19:34.

Third, the study also demonstrated that the imagery of "blood and water" in 19:34 was related to the imagery of "sin and uncleanness" in Zech 13:1 not only conceptually but literarily, through the technical terms "blood of sin" and "water of uncleanness" in the Mosaic Law. The combination of the conceptual and literary associations of this imagery leads to the firm conclusion that a correlation between the imagery of John 19:34 and Zech 13:1 was indeed intended by the author.

Fourth, and finally, the study demonstrated that John 19:34b was related to Zech 14:8 through John 20:19–23. Just as the flow of a purificatory fountain in Zech 13:1 anticipated the flow of "living water" in 14:8, so the flow of "blood and water" in John 19:34b anticipated the flow of the "Holy Spirit" in John 20:19–23.

Though all of the above contributions are significant, the most important contribution is that for which this study was undertaken originally—to provide a comprehensive narrative-critical study of John 19:34. The accomplishment of this has advanced narrative-critical research of Johannine literature.

SUGGESTIONS FOR FUTURE STUDY

Given the contributions noted above, it is anticipated that the present study will assist future research regarding similar imagery to that of John 19:34 in two other NT passages and in Jewish literary traditions regarding the wilderness rock. It is appropriate, therefore, to close this study with a few suggestions in this regard.

In Rev 1:7 the narrator states, "Behold, he is coming with the clouds, and every eye will see him, even those who pierced him; and all the tribes of the land will mourn him . . . ." The passage is a combined allusion to Dan 7:13 and Zech 12:10–14.[4] It is difficult to determine definitively if there is a

4. Ford, *Revelation*, 379–80.

Closing Remarks

direct relationship between John 19:34, 37 and Rev 1:7, but it is evident that Rev 1:7, like John 19:37, associates the death of Jesus with a piercing of his body in fulfillment of Zech 12:10.[5]

Based upon the study's conclusions concerning the use of Zech 12:10 in John 19:37 and the influence of the Zech 13:1 and 14:8 on the imagery of John 19:34, it is worthwhile to investigate whether Zech 13:1 and 14:8 may have comparably influenced the book of Revelation in certain occurrences of the words "blood" (see Rev 1:5; 7:14; 12:11) and "water" (see Rev 7:17; 21:6; 22:1, 17).

Another passage in the NT that shares similar imagery with John 19:34 is 1 John 5:6–8:

> This is the one who came by water and blood, Jesus Christ, not with water alone, but with water and with blood. And the Spirit is the one that testifies, for the Spirit is the truth. So there are three that testify, the Spirit and the water and the blood, and these three agree.[6]

There are a number of interesting similarities between this passage and John 19:34 but the most obvious is the commonality of the elements blood, water, Spirit, and testimony.[7] Given such similarities it is reasonable to surmise that some relationship between the two passages may exist. As Brown has commented, "We do seem to have here two closely related passages from the same school of writing."[8]

In considering the likelihood that there is some relationship, it is interesting to note that there are also significant differences between the two passages. One question that has often troubled exegetes is that if the two passages are indeed related, why is there a difference in the order of the words "blood" and "water"?[9] In the Gospel the words are ordered "blood"

---

5. Though it could be a simple coincidence, the existence of a literary relationship between John 19:37 and Rev 1:7 may be indicated by the occurrence of the verb "to pierce" (ἐκκεντεῖν). As has been pointed out by Ford (*Revelation*, 379), this verb appears nowhere else in the NT except in these two passages, and both passages employ the identical form—3rd person, plural, aorist, indicative, active (ἐξεκέντησαν). As was discussed in chapter 5 of the present study, this verb does not occur in the LXX version of Zech 12:10.

6. Concerning the manuscript variant commonly called the Johannine Comma, see Metzger, *Textual Commentary on the Greek New Testament*, 647–49.

7. Brown, *Gospel According to John*, 2.950.

8. Ibid. See also Barrett, *Gospel According to St. John*, 556.

9. See, for example, the comment in Brown, *Epistles of John*, 578.

Seeing Blood and Water

and "water" (19:34) but in 1 John they are ordered "water" and "blood" three times (5:6a, 6b, 8). Another difference that should be noted is that 1 John 5 does not cite Zech 12:10. Indeed, it does not appear that there is a single allusion anywhere in 1 John to the book of Zechariah. Given the significance of Zech 12:10 for John 19:34, 37 and the significance of the book of Zechariah for the Gospel as a whole, the absence of any apparent influence of Zechariah on 1 John is noteworthy.

As demonstrated in the present study, the symbolic significance and order of the words "blood and water" as they appear in John 19:34 correspond to the content and order of the imagery in Zech 13:1, where the prophetic vision foresees an eschatological fountain that purifies from "sin and uncleanness." Zechariah 13:1 is employed in the Gospel because of its relationship to Zech 12:10, which is explicitly cited as a prophetic utterance fulfilled by the soldier's spear stab (19:34, 37).

But since the spear stab is not mentioned in 1 John, Zech 12:10 is not cited in 1 John. Likewise, since Zech 12:10 is not cited, there is no reason for the literary context of Zech 12:10 to be employed. Accordingly, the order of the imagery in Zech 13:1 (i.e., "sin and uncleanness") has no influence on the order of the words "water" and "blood" in 1 John 5:6–8 and allows for the words "water" and "blood" to be influenced by other considerations.[10] This is certainly something that should be explored further.[11]

Another interesting occurrence of similar imagery to that of John 19:34 is the imagery that appears in the rabbinic traditions regarding the wilderness rock. As discussed in chapter 1, it has often been suggested since John Lightfoot that there might be some relationship between the imagery in John 19:34 and the passages in the rabbinic literature that describe both blood and water (in that order) flowing from the wilderness rock when it was struck by Moses (Num 20:10–13).[12]

---

10. The influence that is most often suggested is the order of the events of Jesus' ministry. That is, the water symbolizes the baptism by John and the blood symbolizes the death on the cross. For more discussion, see the summary of the history of exegesis of this passage in Brown, *Epistles of John*, 575-78.

11. This may also be the reason why the words are ordered differently in the scribal addition in Matt 27:49. The story of a soldier stabbing Jesus with a spear is incorporated into Matthew's crucifixion narrative without any reference to Zech 12:10. Without the presence of Zech 12:10, there is little reason why the order of the words "blood" and "water," when incorporated by the scribe, would be influenced by the order of the words "sin and uncleanness" in Zech 13:1.

12. Lightfoot, *Commentary on the New Testament*, 4. 440. Lightfoot refers to *Shemoth Rabba*, which is more commonly known as *Exod. Rab.* Exod 4:9. The same idea also appears in *Tg. Onq.* Num 20:11.

Closing Remarks

Unfortunately, since the date of the extant literature that contains these traditions is over a century later than the date of the Gospel, it is impossible to determine the nature of the relationship between these traditions and John 19:34. Another approach that might assist in answering this question, however, is to determine first what is behind the development of these rabbinic traditions.

By the time of the formation of the rabbinic literature a tradition had begun to develop relating the wilderness rock to the foundation stone of the temple. This same tradition unites the imagery of the fountain purifying of "sin and uncleanness" in Zech 13:1 with the image of water flowing from the foundation of the temple in Ezek 47:1–12.[13]

Based on the conclusion of the present study regarding (1) the relationship of blood to sin and water to uncleanness in the cultural milieu; (2) the literary relationship of the technical terms "blood of sin" and "water of uncleanness" in the Mosaic Law; and (3) the relationship of the words "sin and uncleanness" in Zech 13:1 to the words "blood and water" in John 19:34, it would be worthwhile to investigate whether the imagery of Zech 13:1 may have comparably influenced the development of the rabbinic tradition about blood and water flowing from the rock in the wilderness. This is certainly an area in rabbinic studies that should be considered for further exploration.

CONCLUSION

The present chapter has summarized the methodology and conclusions of this study, its contributions to the field of biblical studies in general, and Johannine research in particular. It has also made some suggestions for the future study of two other NT passages (Rev 1:7; 1 John 5:6–8) and the rabbinic traditions concerning the wilderness rock. Though there is much more that could and certainly will be said about John 19:34 and the wonderful work that is the Fourth Gospel, this chapter concludes the present study.

The great Johannine scholar Raymond E. Brown once summarized the last line of the Gospel in the following words: "The whole Jesus cannot be captured in the pages of a book, even a book such as the Fourth Gospel."[14] One could say also that neither is it possible to capture the whole

---

13. See discussion of *t. Suk.* 3 in Glasson, *Moses in the Fourth Gospel*, 58–59, and Grelot, "Jean VII, 38," 43–51.

14. Brown, *Gospel of St. John and the Johannine Epistles*, 100.

of the Fourth Gospel in the pages of any study. Nevertheless, it is hoped that this narrative-critical analysis of John 19:34 has captured at least a humble glimpse of what the author of the Fourth Gospel intended the original audience to perceive in this key verse and has faithfully brought the same to light for the study's own intended audience.

Bibliography

ANCIENT AUTHORS

Alcuin of York. *Commentaria in Joannis Evangelium.* PL 100:733–1008.
Alexander Natalis. *In Evangelium Secundum S. Joannem Commentaria.* Edited by J.-P. Migne. *Scripturae Sacrae: Cursus Completus* 23–24. Paris: Imprimerie Catholique, 1840.
Ambrose of Milan. *Explanatio Psalmi 45.* Edited by M. Zelzer. CSEL 64. Vienna: der Österreichischen Akademie der Wissenschaften, 1999.
———. *Expositio evangelii Lucae.* Edited by M. Adriaen and M. Testard. CCL 14. Turnholt: Brepols, 1957.
Apollinaris of Hierapolis. *Chronicon Paschale Praef.* PG 92:79–80.
Augustine of Hippo. *In Iohannis Evangelium: Tractatus 104.* Edited by A. Mayer. CCL 36, 8. Turnholt: Brepols, 1954.
Athanasius. *Expositiones in Psalmos.* PG 27:59–546.
———. *In passionem et cruscem Domini.* PG 28:185–250.
Clement of Rome. *Epistula ad Corinthios.* Edited by A. Jaubert. SC 167. Paris: Cerf, 1971.
Cornelius à Lapide. *Commentaria in Joannem.* Edited by A. Crampon. *Commentaria in Scripturam Sacram R. P. Cornelii a Lapide.* Vol 16. Paris: L. Vives, 1874.
Cyprian of Carthage. *De Rebaptismate.* Edited by G. Hartel. CSEL 3. Vienna: C. Geroldi Filium Bibliopolam Academiae, 1868.
———. *Epistulae.* Edited by G. F. Diercks. CCL IIIc, 3, 2. Turnholt: Brepols, 1996.
Cyril of Alexandria. *Explantio in Epistolam I ad Corinthios.* PG 74:855–914.
Cyril of Jerusalem. *Catechesis.* PG 33:331–1126.
Denis the Carthusian. *Enarratio in Joannis.* Edited by M. Leone. Montreuil, Turin, Parkminster: Typis Cartusiae S. M. de Pratis, 1896–1935.
Epiphanius of Cyprus. *Panarion.* Edited by K. Holl. GCS 31. Leipzig: J. C. Hinrichs'sche Buchhandlung, 1915.
Epistle of Barnabas. Edited by P. Prigent and R. Kraft. SC 172. Paris: Cerf, 1971.
Euripides, *Bacchae.* Edited and Translated by E. R. Dodds. Oxford: Clarendon, 1944.
Hilary of Poitiers. *Tractus Mysteriorum.* Edited by A. Feder. CSEL 64. Vienna: Tempsky, 1916.
Hippolytus of Rome. ΠΕΡΙ ΤΟΥ ΑΝΤΙΧΡΙΣΤΟΥ. Edited by H. Achelis. GCS *Hippolytus Werke* I, 2. Leipzig: J. C. Hinrichs'sche Buchhandlung, 1897.
Ignatius of Antioch. *Epistulae.* Edited by T. Camelot. SC 10. Paris: Cerf, 1969.

Bibliography

Irenaeus of Lyons. *Adversus Haereses*. Edited by A. Rousseau and L. Doutreleau. SC 211. Paris: Cerf, 1974.
John Calvin. *In Evangelium Ioannes*. Edited by G. Baum, E. Cunitz, and E. Reuss. *Corpus Reformatorum* 47. Braunschweig: Schwetschke, 1892.
John Chrysostom. *In Joannem Homiliae*. PG 59:5–482.
John of Damascus. *Expositio Fidei Orthodoxae*. PG 94:790–1219.
———. *Sacra Parallela*. PG 95:1070–1586.
John Scotus Eriugena. *Homilia in prologum Evangelii secundum Joannem*. PL 122:283–346.
Martin Luther. *D. Martin Luthers Werke*. Kritische Gesamtausgabe. 120 vols. Weimar: Herman Böhlaus Nachfolger, 1883–2002.
Philip Melanchton. *Enarratio in Evangelium Joannis*. Edited by C. G. Bretschneider. Corpus Reformatorum 15. Brunsvigae: Appelhans & Pfenningstorff, 1848.
Methodius of Olympia. *Symposion e peri hagneias*. Edited by H. Mursurillo and V. Debidour. SC 95. Paris: Cerf, 1963.
Nicholas of Lyra. *Postilla Super Totam Bibliam*. Facsimile of Strasburg text, 1492. Frankfurt: Minerva G. M. B. H, 1971.
Origen. *Contra Celsum*, Edited by M. Borret. SC 132. Paris: Cerf, 1967.
———. *Homiliae Canticum Canticorum*. PG 13:37–196.
———. *In Exodum Homilia*. Edited by W. A. Baehrens. GCS 29. Leipzig: J. C. Hinrichs'sche Buchhandlung, 1920.
———. *In Iesu Nave Homilia*. Edited by A. Jaubert. SC 71. Paris: Cerf, 1960.
Prudentius. *Dittochaeun*. PL 60:89–112.
———. *Peristephanon*. PL 60: 275–590.
Rupert of Deutz. *Commentaria in Joannem*. PL 169:205–998.
Tertullian. *De Anima*. Edited by J. H. Waszink. Amsterdam: J. M. Meulenhoff, 1947.
———. *De Baptismo*. Edited by B. Luiselli. 2nd ed. Turin: Paravia, 1968.
Theophylactus of Ohrid. *Commentarius in Joannis Evangelium*. PG 124:9–318.
Thomas Aquinas. *Super evangelium S. Ioannis lectura*. Edited by Raffaele Cai. Rome: Marietti, 1952.

MODERN AUTHORS

Aland, Kurt, and Barbara Aland. *The Text of the New Testament: An Introduction to the Critical Editions and to the Theory and Practice of Modern Textual Criticism*. 2nd ed. Grand Rapids, MI: Eerdmans, 1989.
Allison, Dale C. Jr., *The End of the Ages Has Come: An Early Interpretation of the Passion and Resurrection of Jesus*. Philadelphia, PA: Fortress, 1985.
———. "The Living Water (John 4:10–14; 6:35c; 7:37–39)." *St. Vladimir's Theological Quarterly* 30 (1986) 143–57.
Barbet, Pierre. *A Doctor at Calvary*. New York: Doubleday, 1963.
Barnhart, Bruno. *The Good Wine: Reading John the Center*. New York: Paulist, 1993.
Barrett, Charles K. *Essays on John*. Philadelphia, PA: Westminster, 1982.
———. *The Gospel According to St. John: An Introduction with Commentary and Notes on the Greek Text*. London: SPCK, 1955.
Barrosse, Thomas. "The Seven Days of the New Creation in St. John's Gospel." *CBQ* 21 (1959) 507–16.

Bibliography

Bauckham, Richard J. "For Whom Were Gospels Written?" In *The Gospels for all Christians: Rethinking the Gospel Audiences*, edited by Richard Bauckham, 9–48. Grand Rapids, MI: Eerdmans, 1998.

———. *Jesus and the Eyewitnesses: The Gospels as Eyewitness Testimony*. Grand Rapids, MI: Eerdmans, 2006.

———. "The Beloved Disciple as Ideal Author." *JSNT* 49 (1993) 21–44.

———. *The Testimony of the Beloved Disciple: Narrative, History, and Theology in the Gospel of John*. Grand Rapids, MI: Baker, 2007.

Bassler, Jouette M. "Mixed Signals: Nicodemus in the Fourth Gospel." *JBL* 108 (1989) 635–46.

Beck, D. R. "The Narrative Function of Anonymity in Fourth Gospel Characterization." In *Characterization in Biblical Literature*, edited by Elizabeth S. Malbon and A. Berlin, 143–58. *Semeia* 63. Atlanta: Scholars, 1993.

Bernard, John H. *A Critical Commentary on the Gospel According to St. John*. 2 vols. Edited by A. H. McNeile. Edinburgh: T. & T. Clark, 1928.

Bird, Mike. "Bauckham's *The Gospel For All Christians* Revisited." *European Journal of Theology* 15 (2006) 5–13.

Boismard, Marie-Emile. *Du Baptême à Cana: Jean 1:19–2:11*. Paris: Cerf, 1956.

———. "Eau." In *Vocabulaire de Théologie Biblique*, edited by Xavier Léon-Dufour, 235–40. Paris: Cerf, 1966.

Borgen, Peder. *Bread from Heaven: An Exegetical Study of the Concept of Manna in the Gospel of John and the Writings of Philo*. Leiden: Brill, 1965.

Borowski, Oded. "Eat, Drink and Be Merry: The Mediterranean Diet." *Near Eastern Archaeology* 67 (2004) 96–107.

Bouyer, Louis. *The Fourth Gospel*. Westminster, MD: Newman, 1964.

Brock, Sebastian P. "The Mysteries Hidden in the Side of Christ." *Sobernost* 8 (1978) 462–72.

———. "The Wedding Feast of Blood on Golgotha: An Unusual Aspect of John 19, 34 in Syriac Tradition." *The Harp* 6 (1993) 121–34.

Brodie, Thomas L. *The Gospel According to John: A Literary and Theological Commentary*. New York: Oxford University Press, 1993.

Brown, Raymond E. *An Introduction to the New Testament*. ABRL. New York: Doubleday, 1997.

———. *Death of the Messiah: From Gethsemane to the Grave: A Commentary on the Passion Narratives in the Four Gospels*. 2 vols. ABRL. New York: Doubleday, 1994.

———. *Introduction to the Gospel of John*. Edited by Francis J. Moloney. ABRL. New York: Doubleday, 2003.

———. *New Testament Essays*. Garden City, NY: Doubleday, 1968.

———. *The Community of the Beloved Disciple: The Life, Loves, and Hates of an Individual Church in New Testament Times*. New York: Paulist, 1979.

———. *The Epistles of John: Translated with Introduction, Notes and Commentary*. AB 30. New York: Doubleday, 1982.

———. *The Gospel According to John*. 2 vols. AB 29–29a. Garden City, NY: Doubleday, 1966–70.

———. *The Gospel of St. John and the Johannine Epistles: Introduction and Commentary*. 2nd ed. New Testament Reading Guide 13. Collegeville, MN: Liturgical, 1965.

———. "The Johannine Sacramentary Reconsidered." *TS* 23 (1962) 183–206.

Bibliography

Buchanan, George W. "Running Water at the Temple of Zion." *Expository Times* 115 (2004) 289–92.

Bulembat, Matand. "Head-Waiter and Bridegroom of the Wedding at Cana: Structure and Meaning of John 2.1–12." *JSNT* 30 (2007) 55–73.

Bultmann, Rudolf K. *Das Evangelium des Johannes*. KEK. Göttingen: Vandenhoeck & Ruprecht, 1962.

Burge, Gary M. *The Anointed Community: The Holy Spirit in the Johannine Tradition*. Grand Rapids, MI: Eerdmans, 1987.

Burghardt, Walter J. "Did Saint Ignatius of Antioch Know the Fourth Gospel?" *TS* 1 (1940) 1–26, 130–56.

Burridge, Richard A. *What Are the Gospels?: A Comparison with Graeco-Roman Biography*. SNTSMS 70. Cambridge, MA: Cambridge University Press, 1992.

Burrows, Millar, John C. Trever, and William H. Brownlee. *The Dead Sea Scrolls of St. Mark's Monastery*. 2 vols. New Haven, CT: The American Schools of Oriental Research, 1950–51.

Carroll, John T., and Joel B. Green. *The Death of Jesus in Early Christianity*. Peabody, MA: Hendrickson, 1995.

Carson, Donald A. *The Gospel According to John*. Grand Rapids, MI: Eerdmans, 1991.

Carvalho, José C. "The Symbology of 'αἷμα καὶ ὕδωρ' in John 19,34: A Reappraisal." *Didaskalia* 31 (2001) 41–59.

Choksy, Jamsheed. "The Zoroastrian Nahn Purification Rituals." *Journal of Ritual Studies* 1 (1987) 59–74.

Collins, Raymond F. "Cana (Jn. 2:1–12)—The First of His Signs or the Key to His Signs?" *ITQ* 47 (1980) 79–95.

———. "From John to the Beloved Disciple: An Essay on Johannine Characters." *Int* 49 (1995) 359–69.

———. "John's Gospel: A Passion Narrative?" *TBT* 24 (1986) 181–86.

———. "Speaking of the Jews: 'Jews' in the Discourse Material of the Fourth Gospel." In *Anti-Judaism and the Fourth Gospel*, edited by R. Bieringer, D. Pollefeyt, and F. Vandescasteele-Vanneuville, 158–75. Louisville, KY: Westminster John Knox, 2001.

———. *These Things Have Been Written: Studies on the Fourth Gospel*. Louvain Theological & Pastoral Monographs 2. Leuven: Peeters, 1990.

Coloe, Mary L. *God Dwells with Us: Temple Symbolism in the Fourth Gospel*. Collegeville, MN: Liturgical, 2001.

———. "Raising the Johannine Temple." *AusBR* 48 (2000) 47–58.

———. "Welcome into the Household of God: The Foot Washing in John 13." *CBQ* 66 (2004) 400–415.

Connell, Martin F. "*Nisi Pedes*, Except for the Feet: Footwashing in the Community of John's Gospel." *Worship* 70 (1996) 517–31.

Cory, Catherine. "Wisdom's Rescue: A New Reading of the Tabernacles Discourse (John 7:1–8:59)." *JBL* 116 (1997) 95–116.

Crenshaw, James L. *Joel: A New Translation with Introduction and Commentary*. AB 24c. New York: Doubleday, 1995.

Cullmann, Oscar. *Early Christian Worship*. SBT 10. London: SCM, 1953.

Culpepper, R. Alan. *Anatomy of the Fourth Gospel: A Study in Literary Design*. Philadelphia, PA: Fortress, 1983.

———. *John, the Son of Zebedee: The Life of a Legend*. Studies on Personalities in the New Testament. Edited by D. Moody Smith. Columbia, SC: University of South Carolina, 1994.

———. *The Gospel and Letters of John*. Nashville, TN: Abingdon, 1998.

———. "The Johannine *Hypodeigma*: A Reading of John 13." *Semeia* 53 (1991) 133–52.

Cumont, Franz. *After Life in Roman Paganism*. New York: Dover, 1922.

Daise, Michael A. "'If Anyone Thirsts, Let That One Come to Me and Drink': The Literary Texture of John 7:37b-38a." *JBL* 122 (2003) 687–99.

de Boer, Martinus C. "Narrative Criticism, Historical Criticism, and the Gospel of John." *JSNT* 47 (1992) 35–48.

DeLaine, Janet. "Recent Research on Roman Baths." *Journal of Roman Archaeology* 1 (1988) 14–17.

de la Potterie, Ignace. "Le Symbolisme du sang et de l'eau en Jn 19,34." *Didaskalia* 14 (1984) 201–30.

———. *The Hour of Jesus: The Passion and the Resurrection of Jesus According to John*. New York: Alba House, 1989.

Derrett, J. Duncan M. "Water into Wine." *BZ* 7 (1963) 80–97.

Dodd, Charles H. *The Fourth Gospel*. Cambridge, MA: Cambridge University Press, 1953.

Draper, J. A. "Temple, Tabernacle and Mystical Experience in John." *Neot* 31 (1997) 263–88.

du Rand, J. A. "Narratological Perspectives on John 13:1–38." *Hervormde Teologiese Studies* 46 (1990) 367–89.

Eliav, Yaron. "The Roman Bath as a Jewish Institution: Another Look at the Encounter between Judaism and the Greco-Roman Culture." *JSJ* 31 (2000) 416–54.

Enz, Jacob J. "The Book of Exodus as a Literary Type for the Gospel of John." *JBL* 76 (1957) 208–15.

Fagan, Garrett G. "Bathing for Health with Celsus and Pliny the Elder." *Classical Quarterly* 56 (2006) 190–207.

Ferguson, Everett. "Wine as Table-Drink in the Ancient World." *ResQ* 13 (1970) 141–53.

Ferguson, John. *Greek and Roman Religions: A Source Book*. Park Ridge, NJ: Noyes, 1980.

Feuillet, André. *Johannine Studies*. Staten Island, NY: Alba House, 1965.

Fitzmyer, Joseph A. *Paul and His Theology: A Brief Sketch*. 2nd ed. Englewood Cliffs, NJ: Prentice Hall, 1967.

———. "Qumran Literature and the Johannine Writings." In *Life in Abundance: Studies of John's Gospel in Tribute to Raymond E. Brown*, edited by John R. Donahue, 117–33. Collegeville, MN: Liturgical, 2005.

———. *The Dead Sea Scrolls and Christian Origins*. Grand Rapids, MI: Eerdmans, 2000.

Ford, J. Massyngberde. "'Mingled Blood' from the Side of Christ (John XIX.34)." *NTS* 15 (1968–69) 337–38.

———. *Revelation: Introduction, Translation and Commentary*. AB 38; Garden City, NY: Doubleday, 1975.

Franzmann, Majella. "Living Water Mediating Element in Mandaean Myth and Ritual." *Numen* 36 (1989) 156–72.

Freed, Edwin D. *Old Testament Quotations in the Gospel of John*. NovTSup 11. Leiden: Brill, 1965.

Gaster, Theodor H. *Myth, Legend, and Custom in the Old Testament*. New York: Peter Smith, 1975.

Bibliography

Gignac, Francis T. *A Grammar of the Greek Papyri of the Roman and Byzantine Periods*. 2 vols.; Testi e documenti per lo studio dell'antichita 55; Milan: Cisalpino-Goliardica, 1975–81.

———. "The Use of Verbal Variety in the Fourth Gospel." In *Transcending Boundaries: Contemporary Readings of the New Testament*, edited by Rekha M. Chennattu and Mary L. Coloe, 191–200. Rome: LAS, 2005.

Gilders, William K. *Blood Ritual in the Hebrew Bible*. Baltimore, MD: Johns Hopkins University Press, 2004.

Girard, Marc. "La Composition structurelle des sept signes dans le quatrième évangile." *SR* 9 (1980) 315–24.

Glasson, Thomas F. *Moses in the Fourth Gospel*. SBT 40. London: SCM, 1963.

Goodenough, Erwin R. *Jewish Symbols in the Greco-Roman Period*. 6 vols. Bollingen 37. New York: Bollingen Foundation, 1956.

Grassi, Joseph A. "Eating Jesus' Flesh and Drinking His Blood: The Centrality of Meaning of John 6:51–58." *BTB* 17 (1987) 24–30.

———. "The Role of Jesus' Mother in John's Gospel: A Reappraisal." *CBQ* 48 (1986) 67–80.

Grelot, Pierre. "Jean VII, 38: Eau du rocher ou source du Temple." *RB* 70 (1963) 43–51.

Grigsby, Bruce H. "The Cross as an Expiatory Sacrifice in the Fourth Gospel." *JSNT* 15 (1982) 51–80.

Hägerland, Tobias. "John's Gospel: A Two-Level Drama?" *JSNT* 25 (2003) 309–22.

Harrill, J. Albert. "Cannibalistic Language in the Fourth Gospel and Greco-Roman Polemics of Factionalism (John 6:52–66)." *JBL* 127 (2008) 133–58.

Heer, Josef. "The Soteriological Significance of the Johannine Image of the Pierced Savior." In *Faith in Christ and the Worship of Christ*, edited by Leo Scheffczyk, 33–46. San Francisco, CA: Ignatius, 1986.

Heil, John Paul. *Blood and Water: The Death and Resurrection of Jesus in John 18–21*. CBQMS 27. Washington, DC: Catholic Biblical Association, 1995.

Hengel, Martin. "The Interpretation of the Wine Miracle at Cana: John 2:1–11." In *The Glory of Christ in the New Testament: Studies in Christology*, edited by L. D. Hurst and N. T. Wright, 83–112. Oxford: Clarendon, 1987.

———. *The Johannine Question*. Philadelphia, PA: Trinity, 1989.

Henry, Matthew. *Commentary on the Whole Bible*. Peabody, MA: Hendrickson, 2008.

Hidiroglou, Patricia. "Aqueducts, Basins, and Cisterns: The Water Systems at Qumran." *Near Eastern Archaeology* 63 (2000) 138–39.

Hodges, Zane C. "Rivers of Living Water—John 7:37–39." *BSac* 136 (1979) 239–48.

Hoskyns, Edwyn C. *The Fourth Gospel by the Late Edwyn Clement Hoskyns*. Edited by F. N. Davey. 2nd ed. London: Faber & Faber, 1947.

Howard, James M. "The Significance of Minor Characters in the Gospel of John." *BSac* 163 (2006) 63–78.

Hultgren, Arland J. "The Johannine Footwashing (13:1–11) as Symbol of Eschatological Hospitality." *NTS* 28 (1982) 539–46.

Hutchison, John C. "Was John the Baptist an Essene from Qumran?" *BSac* 159 (2002) 187–200.

Jansma, Taeke. *Inquiry into the Hebrew Text and Ancient Versions of Zechariah IX-XIV*. OTS 7. Leiden: Brill, 1949.

Jeremias, Joachim. *The Eucharistic Words of Jesus*. New York: Charles Scribner's Sons, 1966.

Jones, Larry P. *The Symbol of Water in the Gospel of John*. JSNTSup 145. Sheffield: Sheffield Academic Press, 1997.
Keener, Craig S. *The Gospel of John: A Commentary*. 2 vols. Peabody, MA: Hendrickson, 2003.
———. *The Spirit in the Gospels and Acts: Divine Purity and Power*. Peabody, MA: Hendrickson, 1997.
Kilpatrick, George D. "John 4:9." *JBL* 87 (1968) 327–28.
———. "Some Notes on Johannine Usage." *BT* 11 (1960) 173–77.
———. *The Eucharist in Bible and Liturgy*. Cambridge, MA: Cambridge University Press, 1983.
———. "The Punctuation of John VII. 37–38." *JTS* 11 (1960) 340–42.
———. "The Religious Background of the Fourth Gospel." In *Studies in the Fourth Gospel*, edited by F. L. Cross, 36–44. London: A. R. Mowbray, 1957.
Kim, Stephen S. "The Relationship of John 1:19–51 to the Book of Signs in John 2–12." *BSac* 165 (2008) 323–37.
Kingsbury, Jack D. "Reflections on 'the Reader' of Matthew's Gospel." *NTS* 34 (1988) 442–60.
Kleinig, John W. "The Blood for Sprinkling: Atoning Blood in Leviticus and Hebrews." *Lutheran Theological Journal* 33 (1999) 124–35.
Klink, Edward W. "The Gospel Community Debate: State of the Question." *Currents in Biblical Research* 3 (2004) 60–85.
Kodell, Jerome. *The Eucharist in the New Testament*. Collegeville, MN: Liturgical, 1988.
Koester, Craig R. *Symbolism in the Fourth Gospel: Meaning, Mystery, Community*. 2nd ed. Minneapolis, MN: Fortress, 2003.
Kysar, Robert. "The Whence and Whither of the Johannine Community." In *Life in Abundance: Studies of John's Gospel in Tribute to Raymond E. Brown*, edited by John R. Donahue, 65–81. Collegeville, MI: Liturgical, 2005.
Lagrange, Marie-Joseph. *Évangile selon Saint Jean*. EBib. 5th ed. Paris: Gabalda, 1936.
Levine, Baruch A. *Numbers: A New Translation with Introduction and Commentary*. AB 4–4A. New York: Doubleday, 1993–2000.
Lightfoot, Robert H. *St. John's Gospel: A Commentary*. Ed. C. F. Evans; Oxford: Oxford University Press, 1956.
Lightfoot, John. *A Commentary on the New Testament from the Talmud and Hebraica*. Translated by R. Gandell. 4 vols. Oxford: Oxford University Press, 1859. Reprint, Peabody, MA: Hendrickson, 1989.
Lincoln, Andrew T. *The Gospel According to Saint John*. BNTC 4. London: Continuum, 2005.
Little, Edmund. *Echoes of the Old Testament in the Wine of Cana in Galilee (John 2:1–11) and The Multiplication of the Loaves and Fish (John 6:1–15): Towards an Appreciation*. CahRB 41. Paris: Gabalda, 1998.
———. "The Scandal of Cana: A Regrettable Miracle." *Stimulus* 16 (2008) 23–30.
Macgregor, G. H. C. "The Eucharist in the Fourth Gospel." *NTS* 9 (1962) 111–19.
———. *The Gospel of John*. New York: Harper, 1928.
Maertens, Thierry. *A Feast in Honor of Yahweh*. Notre Dame, IN: Fides, 1965.
Magen, Yitzhak. "Ancient Israel's Stone Age: Purity in Second Temple Times." *BARev* 24 (1998) 46–52.

Bibliography

Maguire, Alban A. *Blood and Water: The Wounded Side of Christ in Early Christian Literature*. Studies in Sacred Theology 108. Washington, DC: Catholic University of America, 1956.

Malatesta, Edward. "Blood and Water from the Pierced Side of Christ." In *Segni e Sacramenti nel Vangelo di Giovanni*, edited by P.-R. Tragan, 164-81. Studia Anselmiana 66. Rome: Anselmiana, 1977.

Malina, Bruce J., and Richard L. Rohrbaugh. *Social-Science Commentary on the Gospel of John*. Minneapolis, MN: Fortress, 1998.

Marcus, Joel. "Rivers of Living Water From Jesus' Belly (John 7:38)." *JBL* 117 (1998) 328-30.

Maritz, Petrus. "The Imagery of Eating and Drinking in John 6:35." In *Imagery in the Gospel of John*, edited by Jörg Frey, Jan G. van der Watt, and Ruben Zimmermann, 333-52. WUNT 200. Tübingen: Mohr Siebeck, 2006.

Martyn, J. Louis. *History and Theology in the Fourth Gospel*. New York: Harper and Row, 1968.

Matera, Frank J. *New Testament Christology*. Louisville, KY: Westminster John Knox, 1999.

——. *New Testament Theology: Exploring Diversity and Unity*. Louisville, KY: Westminster John Knox, 2007.

Matthews, Victor H. "Treading the Winepress: Actual and Metaphorical Viticulture in the Ancient Near East." *Semeia* 86 (1999) 19-32.

McNally, Robert. *The Bible in the Early Middle Ages*. Edited by John C. Murray and Walter J. Burghardt. Woodstock Papers 4. Westminster, MD: Newman, 1959.

Meehan, Thomas M. "John 19:32-35 and 1 John 5:6-8: A Study in the History of Interpretation." Ph.D. diss., Drew University, Madison, NJ, 1985.

Meeks, Wayne A. "The Man from Heaven in Johannine Sectarianism." *JBL* 91 (1972) 44-72.

Meier, John P. *A Marginal Jew: Rethinking the Historical Jesus*. 4 vols. ABRL. New York: Doubleday, 1991-2009.

——. "John the Baptist in Matthew's Gospel." *JBL* 99 (1980) 383-405.

Menken, Maarten J. J. "John 6:51c-58: Eucharist or Christology." In *Critical Readings of John 6*, edited by R. Alan Culpepper, 183-204. Biblical Interpretation Series 22. Leiden: Brill, 1992.

——. *Old Testament Quotations in the Fourth Gospel: Studies in Textual Form*. CBET 15. Kampen, Netherlands: Kok Pharos, 1998.

Metzger, Bruce M. *A Textual Commentary on the Greek New Testament*, 2nd ed. Stuttgart: German Bible Society, 1994.

——. *The Text of the New Testament: Its Transmission, Corruption, and Restoration*. New York: Oxford University Press, 1964.

Meyers, Carol L., and Eric M. Meyers. "Jerusalem and Zion After the Exile: The Evidence of First Zechariah." In *"Sha'arei Talmon": Studies in the Bible, Qumran, and the Ancient Near East Presented to Shemaryahu Talmon*, edited by M. Fishbane and E. Tov, 121-35. Winona Lake, IN: Eisenbrauns, 1992.

——. *Zechariah 9-14: A New Translation with Introduction and Commentary*. AB 25c. New York: Doubleday, 1993.

Michaels, J. Ramsey. "By Water and Blood: Sin and Purification in John and First John." In *Dimensions of Baptism: Biblical and Theological Studies*, edited by Stanley E. Porter and Anthony R. Cross, 149-62. JSNTSup 234. London: Sheffield, 2002.

——. *John*. Peabody, MA: Hendrickson, 1984.

Bibliography

Miguens, M. "'Salió sangre y agua' (Jn. 19,34)." *SBFLA* 14 (1963–64) 5–31.
Milgrom, Jacob. *Leviticus: A New Translation with Introduction and Commentary.* 2 vols. AB 3–3a. New York: Doubleday, 1991–2000.
Miller, Robert P. "τί ἐμοὶ καὶ σοί: John 2:4—Rebuke or Expression of Mutual Concern?" Ph.D. diss., The Catholic University of America, Washington, DC, 2009.
Minear, Paul S. *John: The Martyr's Gospel.* New York: Pilgrim, 1984.
Mitchell, Margaret M. "Patristic Counter-Evidence to the Claim That 'The Gospels Were Written for All Christians.'" *NTS* 51 (2005) 36–79.
Mlakuzhyil, George. *The Christocentric Literary Structure of the Fourth Gospel.* AnBib 117. Rome: Biblical Institute, 1987.
Moloney, Francis J. "The Function of Prolepsis in the Interpretation of John 6." In *Critical Readings of John 6*, edited by R. Alan Culpepper, 129–48. Biblical Interpretation Series 22. Leiden: Brill, 1992.
———. *The Gospel of John.* SacPag 4. Collegeville, MN: Liturgical, 1998.
———. *The Johannine Son of Man.* Biblioteca di Scienze Religiose 14. 2nd ed. Rome: LAS, 1978.
———. "The Structure and Message of John 13:1–38." *AusBR* 34 (1986) 1–16.
———. "When is John Talking about Sacraments." *AusBR* 28 (1980) 10–33.
Morris, Leon. *Studies in the Fourth Gospel.* Grand Rapids, MI: Eerdmans, 1969.
———. *The Gospel According to John.* 2nd ed. Grand Rapids, MI: Eerdmans, 1995.
Neusner, Jacob. *Symbol and Theology in Early Judaism.* Minneapolis, MN: Fortress, 1991.
———. *The Tosefta: An Introduction.* Florida Studies in the History of Judaism 47. Atlanta: Scholars, 1992.
Ng, Wai-yee. *Water Symbolism in John: An Eschatological Interpretation.* Studies in Biblical Literature 15. New York: Lang, 2001.
Nielsen, Jesper T. "The Lamb of God: The Cognitive Structure of a Johannine Metaphor." In *Imagery in the Gospel of John*, edited by Jörg Frey, Jan G. van der Watt, and Ruben Zimmermann, 217–56. WUNT 200. Tübingen: Mohr Siebeck, 2006.
Neyrey, Jerome H. *The Gospel of John.* New Cambridge Bible Commentary. Cambridge: Cambridge University Press, 2007.
Nongbri, Brent. "The Use and Abuse of P52: Papyrological Pitfalls in the Dating of the Fourth Gospel." *HTR* 98 (2005) 23–48.
O'Day, Gail R. "Toward a Narrative-Critical Study of John." *Int* 49 (1995) 341–46.
Olsson, Birger. *Structure and Meaning in the Fourth Gospel: A Text Linguistic Analysis of John 2:1–11 and 4:1–42.* ConBNT 6. Lund: Gleerup, 1974.
Pamment, Margaret. "John 3:5." *NovT* 25 (1983) 189–90.
Pennells, Stephen. "The Spear Thrust (Mt 27:49b, v.l. / Jn 19:34)." *JSNT* 19 (1983) 99–115.
Pollard, T. E. *Johannine Christology and the Early Church.* Cambridge, MA: Cambridge University Press, 1970.
Powell, Mark A. *What is Narrative Criticism?* Minneapolis, MN: Fortress, 1990.
Primrose, W. B. "A Surgeon Looks at the Crucifixion." *Hibbert Journal* 47 (1949) 383–88.
Propp, William H. C. *Exodus: A New Translation with Introduction and Commentary.* AB 2–2A. New York: Doubleday, 1999–2006.
Pryor, John W. "John 3.3,5. A Study in the Relation of John's Gospel to the Synoptic Tradition." *JSNT* 41 (1991) 71–95.
Quasten, Johannes. *Patrology I and II.* Utrecht: Spectrum, 1950. Reprint, Allen, TX: Christian Classics, 1983.

Bibliography

Reeves, John C. "The Feast of the First Fruits of Wine and the Ancient Canaanite Calendar." *VT* 42 (1992) 350–61.
Richardson, Peter. "What Has Cana to Do with Capernaum." *NTS* 48 (2002) 314–31.
Richter, Georg. "Blut und Wasser aus der durchbohrten Seite Jesu (Joh 19,34b)." *MTZ* 21 (1970) 1–21.
Ridderbos, Herman. *The Gospel of John: A Theological Commentary*. Grand Rapids, MI: Eerdmans, 1997.
Ryle, John C. *Expository Thoughts on the Gospels*. 3 vols. Cambridge, England: Clarke, 1985. First published in 1856.
Sava, Anthony F. "The Wound in the Side of Christ." *CBQ* 19 (1957) 343–46.
———. "The Wounds of Christ." *CBQ* 16 (1954) 438–43.
Sawyer, Deborah. F. "Water and Blood: Birthing Images in John's Gospel." In *Words Remembered, Texts Renewed: Essays in Honour of John F.A. Sawyer*, edited by John Davies, Graham Harvey, and Wilfred G.E. Watson, 300–309. JSOTSup 195. Sheffield: Sheffield Academic Press, 1995.
Schaefer, Konrad R. "Zechariah 14: A Study in Allusion." *CBQ* 57 (1995) 66–91.
Schnackenburg, Rudolf. *Das Johannesevangelium: Einleitung und Kommentar*. 3 vols. HTKNT 4. Freiburg: Herder, 1967.
Schneiders, Sandra M. "The Foot Washing (John 13:1–20): An Experiment in Hermeneutics." *CBQ* 43 (1981) 76–92.
Sesboüé, Daniel. "Vin." In *Vocabulaire de Théologie Biblique*, edited by Xavier Léon-Dufour, 1114–16. Paris: Cerf, 1966.
Sheeley, Steven M. "Nothing (a)B(o)ut the Blood: Images of Jesus' Death in the New Testament." *Perspectives in Religious Studies* 35 (2008) 109–19.
Sim, David C. "The Gospels for all Christians: A Response to Richard Bauckham." *JSNT* 84 (2001) 3–27.
Smith, Derwood. "Jewish Proselyte Baptism and the Baptism of John." *ResQ* 25 (1982) 13–32.
Smith, D. Moody. *John among the Gospels*. 2nd ed. Columbia, SC: University of South Carolina Press, 2001.
Smit, Peter-Ben. "Cana-to-Cana or Galilee-to-Galilee." *ZNW* 98 (2007) 143–49.
Spicq, Ceslas, and Pierre Grelot. "Sang." In *Vocabulaire de Théologie Biblique*, edited by Xavier Léon-Dufour, 994–97. Paris: Cerf, 1966.
Staley, Jeffrey L. *The Print's First Kiss: A Rhetorical Investigation of the Implied Reader in the Fourth Gospel*. SBLDS 82. Atlanta: Scholars, 1988.
Stanley, Phillip V. "Gradation of Quality of Wines in the Greek and Roman Worlds." *Journal of Wine Research* 10 (1999) 105–14.
Stern, Menahem. *Greek and Latin Authors on Jews and Judaism*. 3 vols. Jerusalem: Israel Academy of Sciences and Humanities, 1976.
Stibbe, Mark W. G. *John as Storyteller: Narrative Criticism and the Fourth Gospel*. SNTSMS 73. Cambridge, MA: Cambridge University Press, 1992.
Stroud, William. *A Treatise on the Physical Cause of the Death of Christ*. London: Hamilton and Adams, 1871.
Tabory, Joseph. "The Crucifixion of the Paschal Lamb." *JQR* 86 (1996) 395–406.
Thiering, Barbara E. "Qumran and New Testament Baptism." *NTS* 26 (1980) 266–77.
Thomas, John C. *Footwashing in John 13 and the Johannine Community*. JSNTSup 61. Sheffield: JSOT, 1991.

Bibliography

Toussaint, Stanley D. "The Significance of the First Sign in John's Gospel." *BSac* 134 (1977) 45–51.
Tromp, S. "Nativitas Ecclesiae Ex Corde Iesu in Cruce." *Gregorianum* 13 (1932) 489–527.
Tuckett, Christopher. "Zech 12:10 and the New Testament." In *The Book of Zechariah and Its Influence*, edited by Christopher Tuckett, 111–21. Burlington, VT: Ashgate, 2003.
Vellanickal, Matthew. "Blood and Water." *Jeevadhara* 8 (1978) 219–30.
Visotzky, Burton L. "Methodological Considerations in the Study of John's Interactions with First-Century Judaism." In *Life in Abundance: Studies of John's Gospel in Tribute to Raymond E. Brown*, edited by John R. Donahue, 91–107. Collegeville, MN: Liturgical, 2005.
Webster, Jane S. *Ingesting Jesus: Eating and Drinking in the Gospel of John*. SBL Academia Biblica 6. Atlanta: SBL, 2003.
Wernberg-Møller, Preben, *The Manual of Discipline: Translated and Annotated with an Introduction*. STDJ 1. Grand Rapids, MI: Eerdmans, 1957.
Westcott, Brooke F. *The Gospel According to St. John: The Authorized Version with Introduction and Notes*. London: John Murray, 1892.
Whitaker, Edward C. *Documents of the Baptismal Liturgy*. London: SPCK, 1970.
Wild, Robert A. *Water in the Cultic Worship of Isis and Sarapis*. EPRO 87. Leiden: Brill, 1981.
Wilkinson, John. "The Incident of the Blood and Water in John 19.34." *SJT* 28 (1975) 149–72.
Williams, Rita H. "The Mother of Jesus at Cana: A Social-Science Interpretation of John 2:1–12." *CBQ* 59 (1997) 679–92.
Wiseman, James. "Bacchic Mysteries." *Arch* 54 (2001) 10–14.
Ziegler, Joseph. *Duodecim prophetae*. Septuaginta: Vetus Testamentum Graecum 13. Göttingen: Vandenhoeck & Ruprecht, 1984.

Scripture Index

OLD TESTAMENT

Genesis

1:2	6
4:10	32
4:10–11	24
9:4	24, 35
9:5	24
9:5–6	24
18:4	27, 58
19:2	27, 59
22	35n10
24:32	27, 59
26:19	52n36
27:28	27
43:24	59
49:11	2
49:11–12	47

Exodus

12	35
12:7–13	25
12:10	64
12:16	63
12:22	35
12:22–27	25
12:46	64
15:24	33
16:2	33
16:7–8	33
16:15–16	33n5
17:1–6	55
17:1–7	1, 82
17:1–17	55
17:3	33
19:10, 14	4n13
22:1	32
23:16	55
24:3–8	25
24:6	4n13
29:4	27
29:38–42	35n10
30:10	26n15
30:19	59, 59n54
40:12	27

Leviticus

4:25	26n15
4:34	26n15
5:9	26n15
11:40	27
12:4, 5, 7	32
14:4	25n11
14:5–6	52
14:6	25n11
14:6–7	4n13

Scripture Index

Leviticus (*continued*)

14:8–9	27
14:49	25n11
14:50–52	52
14:51	25n11
14:52	25n11
15	27
15:13	52
16:4	27
16:15–21	25
17:11	24, 25, 66, 83
17:14	24
20:18	32
23:42–43	55
24:4	32
24:5	32
24:7	32
26:3–10	27
26:4	27

Numbers

9:12	64
11:1	33
14:2	33
14:27	33
14:29	33
14:36	33
16:11	33
16:41	33
17:5	33
19:6	25n11
19:6–9	4n13
19:9	27n18, 73n36
19:13	27n18, 73n36
19:17	27n18, 52, 73n36
19:18	4n13, 25n11
19:20	4n13, 27n18, 73n36
19:21	27n18, 73n36
20:2–13	2, 55, 82
20:10–13	90
20:11	4
21:5	33
21:16	55
31:23	27n18, 73n36

Deuteronomy

1:27	33
8:3	33
8:8	47
11:14	27, 47
12:16	24, 35
12:23	24, 35
15:23	24, 35
17:15	64
18:15–18	55
21:22–23	63, 64n6
28:12	27

Joshua

2:18	2, 82
8:29	63

Judges

19:21	59

1 Samuel

14:32–35	24, 35
25:41	59

2 Samuel

11:8	59
21:1	24

Job

5:10	27
12:15	27
28:26	27

Scripture Index

Psalms
33:21	64
34:20	64
41:9	36n12
51:7	25n11, 43
78:5–8	33
78:22	33
78:24	33
79:10	24
104:10–16	27
106:25	33
133:3	27

Proverbs
3:10	47
3:19–20	27

Canticle of Canticles
4:15	52n36

Wisdom
7:2	32

Sirach
24:21	33

Isaiah
4:4	43
25:6	47
30:23–25	27
35:6–7	28
41:17–20	28
44:3–5	28
44:27	27
49:10	28
53:7	35n10
53:10–12	35n10

Jeremiah
5:24	27
31:9	28
31:12	47
33:8	43

Ezekiel
16:6	32
16:9	32
24:7–8	24
31:15	27
34:26	27
35:6	24
36:24–27	28
36:25	73n36
36:25–36	43
36:29	73n36
45:18–20	25n11
45:19	26n15
47:1	53, 56
47:1–12	28, 91
47:8–9	53, 56
47:9	73n36

Daniel
7:13	38, 88

Joel
2:19	47
2:28	28
3:18	28
4:18	53, 56

Amos
9:14	47

Zechariah
9:9	69

Scripture Index

Zechariah (*continued*)
9:11	25
9:17	47
9–14	70
11	69
12:10	65n10, 69, 70, 71, 71n32, 72, 73, 74, 80, 81, 85, 86, 87, 89, 90, 90n11
12:10–14	88
13:1	28, 57, 70, 71, 71n32, 72, 72n33, 73, 73n35, 74, 75, 79, 81, 85, 86, 87, 89, 90, 90n11, 91
13:7	69
14:1	57
14:8	28, 53, 56, 57, 69, 73, 73n35, 74, 75, 77, 81, 85, 86, 87, 88, 89
14:16	57
14:16–17	69
14:17	56n50
14:21	69

2 Maccabees
8:3	24

NEW TESTAMENT

Matthew
3:13–17	28
17:1	13
23:30	26, 39
23:35	26, 39
24:30	38
26:28	26, 36
26:64	38
27:4	26, 39
27:6	26, 39
27:8	26, 39
27:24	26, 39
27:25	26, 39
27:49	1n1, 90n11

Mark
1:9–11	28
5:37	13
9:2	13
13:26	38
14:24	26, 36
14:25	37
14:33	13
14:62	38

Luke
3:21–22	28
7:44	59
8:51	13
9:28	13
11:50	26, 39
11:51	26, 39
13:1	26, 39
21:27	38
22:8	13
22:18	38
22:20	26, 36

John
1:1–3	31
1:1–18	23
1:4–8	31
1:9–10	31
1:11	31
1:12	31, 32, 33, 59n58
1:13	31, 32, 39, 66, 84
1:14	33, 35, 53

Scripture Index

1:19	50	4:5–6	50
1:19–34	28	4:6	50
1:19—12:50	23	4:7	41, 50, 52, 60, 67, 84
1:25	43n7		
1:26	41, 42, 43n7, 49, 60, 67, 84	4:7–15	50, 56
		4:8	50
1:28	43n7	4:9	51, 51n34, 52
1:29	35, 35n10	4:10	41, 51, 52, 60, 67, 74, 84, 86
1:31	41, 42, 43n7, 49, 60, 67, 84	4:10–11	56, 69
1:33	41, 42, 43n7, 49, 57, 60, 67, 75, 79, 84, 86	4:11	41, 51, 51n35, 60, 67, 74, 84
		4:12	51, 52
1:36	35n10	4:13	41, 51, 52, 60, 67, 84
2:1–11	44		
2:1-12	46	4:14	41, 52, 53, 60, 67, 84
2:3–4	45		
2:4	45, 47	4:15	41, 52, 60, 67, 84
2:6	45	4:16–42	52
2:7	41, 45, 46, 60, 67, 84	4:20	53
		4:20–24	76, 86
2:7–9	44	4:21	45
2:8	45	4:23	37, 45, 47
2:9	41, 46, 60, 67, 84	4:24	86
2:10	47, 48	4:46	41, 60, 67, 84
2:11	48	5:7	41, 53n42
2:13–22	56	5:25	37, 45, 47
2:16	69	5:28	45
2:19–22	53	6:4	32
2:23	44	6:16–25	42n2
3:1–15	48	6:24	32
3:2	48	6:25–59	32
3:3	6, 48	6:31	33
3:4	48	6:31–40	55
3:5	36, 41, 44, 49, 57, 60, 67, 75, 76, 77, 79, 84, 86	6:35	33
		6:41	33
		6:49	33
3:14–15	38, 77	6:49–51	55
3:22	49	6:51	33, 35
3:22–4:3	28	6:51–58	36, 76
3:23	41, 43n7, 49, 50, 60, 67, 84	6:52	34, 35
		6:53	34, 35, 36n12, 38, 77
3:25	43, 50		
3:26	50	6:53–56	6, 32, 37, 39, 66, 84

109

Scripture Index

John (*continued*)

6:54	34, 35, 36n12, 37, 77
6:55	34, 34n8, 35, 77
6:56	34, 35, 36n12, 38, 77
6:57	36n12
6:58	36n12
6:59	32
6:61	33
6:62	39, 77
6:63	79, 86
7:13	54
7:30	45
7:32	33
7:37	54, 54n43, 56, 63
7:37–38	54n43
7:37–39	44, 53, 54n43, 63, 69, 75n38, 81, 86
7:38	41, 54, 54n43, 56, 60, 67, 74, 84
7:38–39	5, 7, 44, 76
7:39	54, 57, 63, 74, 75, 85, 86
7:40	55
8:20	45
8:28	38
9:1–4	58n52
10:38	38
10:40	43n7
11:25	37, 47
12:23	45
12:27	45
12:32–34	38
13	59n58
13:1	45
13:1–3	58, 59
13:1—17:26	23
13:1—20:31	23
13:5	41, 58, 60, 67, 84
13:6	58
13:8	58
13:10	58, 59
13:10–11	59
13:12	58
13:14	58
13:18	36n12
13:23	14
14:10–11	38
14:15–17	57
16:32	69
17:1	45
17:24	45
18:1–27	23
18:1–19:42	23
18:18	65
18:28–19:11	23
18:31–33	12
18:37–38	12
19:4	65
19:6	65
19:12–22	23
19:12–42	1, 9, 23
19:14	63
19:15	64
19:23–24	23
19:25–27	23
19:27	45
19:28–30	23
19:31	20, 22, 23, 63, 63, 64n7
19:31–33	24
19:31–37	1, 9, 19, 20, 21, 23, 62, 80, 83, 85
19:32	21, 22, 23, 64
19:32–35	1n1
19:33	21, 22, 64
19:34	1, 21, 22, 36, 41, 64, 65, 65n10, 66, 67, 68, 69, 72, 74, 75, 75n39, 76, 77, 78, 80, 81, 83, 84, 86, 88, 89, 90, 91
19:35	21, 22, 24, 64
19:35–37	24
19:36	21, 22, 23, 24, 64

Scripture Index

19:37	21, 22, 23, 24, 61, 65, 65n10, 69, 70, 71n32, 81, 89, 89n5, 90	6:19–20	57
		10:1–4	28
		10:4	4, 55n44
		10:16	36
19:38–42	23, 65	10:16–18	26, 39
20:1–29	23	11:25	26
20:19–23	63n4, 74, 81, 88	11:25–27	36
20:20	75, 86	11:26	37
20:21–23	57	12:12–13	28, 43, 49, 66, 84
20:21–24	75		
20:22–23	75, 79, 86		
21:1-7	42n2	**Galatians**	
21:1–25	23	2:9	13
21:18–19	12	3:13	64n6
21:20	14		
21:22–23	13, 13n56	**Ephesians**	
21:22–24	13n55	1:7	26, 39
21:24	14, 64n8	2:13–14	39
		5:26	28

Acts of the Apostles

1:19	26, 39	**Colossians**	
3–4	13	1:20–22	39
5:28	26, 39		
5:30	64n6	**1 Timothy**	
6:14	13	5:10	59
10:37–38	28		
10:39	64n6	**Titus**	
13:29	64n6	3:5	28, 43, 49, 66, 84
18:6	26, 39		
20:26	26, 39	**Hebrews**	
22:20	26, 39	9:11–14	26, 66, 83
		9:19	4, 5, 6
Romans		9:22	26
3:15	26, 39	9:23–28	26, 66, 83
3:24–25	26, 39	10:19	26
		10:22	28
1 Corinthians		12:24	26
3:16	57	13:12	26
5:7	26, 35, 39		
6:11	28, 84		
6:12–13	66		

Scripture Index

1 Peter

1:2	26
1:3	49
1:19	26, 35, 39
2:5	57
2:24	64n6
3:21	28

1 John

1:7	26
5:6	90
5:6–8	1n1, 3, 89, 90, 91
5:6–9	3
5:8	90

Revelation

1:5	26, 89
1:7	1n1, 38, 88, 89, 89n5, 91
6:10	26, 39
7:14	26, 89
7:17	89
12:11	26, 89
14:14	38
16:3	26, 39
16:6	26, 39
17:6	26, 39
18:24	26, 39
19:2	26, 39
21:6	89
22:1	89
22:17	89

www.ingramcontent.com/pod-product-compliance
Lightning Source LLC
Chambersburg PA
CBHW050839160426
43192CB00011B/2089